New Edition

This Is Japan

Your Culture, Your Life

Simon Capper

NATIONAL
GEOGRAPHIC
LEARNING

Australia · Brazil · Mexico · Singapore · United Kingdom · United States

This Is Japan, New Edition — Your Culture, Your Life

Simon Capper

© 2021 Cengage Learning K.K.

Photo Credits:
cover: © The Asahi Shimbun/The Asahi Shimbun/Getty Images; 10: © SDI Productions/iStock.com; 11: (t, l to r) © LightFieldStudios/iStock.com, © FG Trade/iStock.com, © dimarik/iStock.com, © ElNariz/iStock.com, (b, l to r) © FG Trade/iStock.com, © drbimages/iStock.com, © recep-bg/iStock.com, © kali9/iStock.com; 16: © kinpouge05/iStock.com; 22: © TanawatPontchour/iStock.com; 26: © viennetta/iStock.com; 28: © Simon Capper; 29: (t, l to r) © Simon Capper, © Simon Capper, © shimikenta/iStock.com, © Archives21/Pacific Press Service, (m, l to r) © Archives21/Pacific Press Service, © jpskenn/iStock.com, © oasis2me/iStock.com, © the8monkey/iStock.com, (b, l to r) © kumikomini/iStock.com, © GI15702993/iStock.com, © Simon Capper, © miura-makoto/iStock.com; 32: © Peter Fleming/iStock.com; 34: © kumikomini/iStock.com; 38: © Simon Capper; 40: © KUOCHUAN CHENG/iStock.com; 41: (t, l to r) © gyro/iStock.com, © lendy16/iStock.com, © Simon Capper, © MindStorm-inc/iStock.com, (mt, l to r) © coward_lion/iStock.com, © tanukiphoto/iStock.com, © NorGal/iStock.com, © shingopix/iStock.com, (mb, l to r) © Simon Capper, © kuppa_rock/iStock.com, © gyro/ iStock.com, © agcuesta/iStock.com, (b, l to r) © Simon Capper, © kuppa_rock/iStock.com, © akiyoko/iStock.com, © freestylephoto/iStock.com; 44: © zepp1969/iStock.com; 48: © kumikomini/iStock.com; 51: (t, l to r) © JohnnyGreig/iStock.com, © Sam Spicer/Moment/Getty Images, (m, l to r) © fototrav/ iStock.com, © NicolasMcComber/iStock.com, (b, l to r) © NicolasMcComber/iStock.com, © davidf/iStock.com; 54: © Tuayai/ iStock.com; 58: © Deborah McPhail/iStock.com; 60: © Drazen_/ iStock.com; 64: © trabantos/iStock.comd; 66: (l) © Kyodo News/Kyodo News/Getty Images, (r) © Masterpress/Getty Images Sport/Getty Images; 70: © Bet_Noire/iStock.com; 72: © Carmen Romero/iStock.com; 73: (t, l to r) © imagenavi/iStock.com, © Simon Capper, © GA161076/ iStock.com, © kharps/iStock.com, (b, l to r) © Jiji Press Photo, © Simon Capper, © Simon Capper, © Simon Capper; 76: © Simon Capper; 78: © imagean/iStock.com; 83: © JohnnyGreig/iStock.com; 97: © Simon Capper

For permission to use material from this textbook or product, e-mail to **eltjapan@cengage.com**

ISBN: 978-4-86312- 383-0

National Geographic Learning | Cengage Learning K.K.
No. 2 Funato Building 5th Floor
1-11-11 Kudankita, Chiyoda-ku
Tokyo 102-0073
Japan

Tel: 03-3511-4392
Fax: 03-3511-4391

Contents

To the Student ··· 4

How to Use This Textbook ·· 6

How to Access the Audio Online ·· 7

Introduction ··· 8

Unit 1   Getting to Know You ·· 10

Unit 2   My Hometown ··· 16

Unit 3   Japanese Food ·· 22

Unit 4   The Traditional Japanese House ··· 28

Unit 5   The Japanese Language ·· 34

Unit 6   Explaining Japanese Things ··· 40

Review Game Units 1–6 ··· 46

Unit 7   Good Manners, Bad Manners ·· 48

Unit 8   Special Days and Events ··· 54

Unit 9   School and University Life ··· 60

Unit 10   Famous Japanese People and Movies ·· 66

Unit 11   Visiting Temples and Shrines ··· 72

Unit 12   Invisible Culture ·· 78

Review Game Units 7–12 ··· 84

Appendix I: Communication Bingo Grids ··· 88

Appendix II: Worksheets for Your Turn and Get Ready ·· 96

To the Student

The idea for *This Is Japan* began many years ago, when some of my students went to do homestays in the UK. They had a great time there, but they were often embarrassed, because they couldn't answer many of the questions that their homestay families asked them. Sometimes they lacked language, and sometimes they lacked knowledge. When they returned to Japan, I started making worksheets that would help them to explain about their lifestyles and culture.

I thought these topics would be easy for them, but actually it was quite challenging. My students had visited many temples and shrines, but had never stopped to think about the differences between Shinto and Buddhism. They used *kanji*, *hiragana* and *katakana* every day, but never stopped to think about how to explain them. People asked them about wedding ceremonies and funerals, but many of the students hadn't yet experienced these events.

Little by little, the worksheets became longer and the topics became deeper. Little by little my students became more confident in their ability to explain—not just to answer questions, but to give more information, and to actively teach their non-Japanese friends about the wonderful culture and customs of Japan.

This Is Japan will help you to explain the Japanese lifestyle and culture more fluently in English. Being able to communicate about your culture will open doors to new friendships and new experiences. I hope you enjoy using this book and that it brings you closer to your classmates and friends. Good luck with your language learning.

- -

When you are using *This Is Japan*, remember the advice on the next page. Check (✓) each box to show that you have read and understood the advice.

☐ **Paraphrase!**	Try not to use your dictionary in face-to-face communication. Sometimes it will be difficult to explain yourself clearly, but try to stay in English, and learn to **paraphrase** (explain using other words, talk your way around a problem).
☐ **Prepare!**	**Prepare** as much as you can. Ask your teacher for the *This Is Japan* workbook and use it to prepare for class.
☐ **Don't rush!**	Don't race through the activities—it's not a competition to see who can finish first—**the winner is the one who communicates best**.
☐ **Say more!**	Don't just give short answers—always try to **give more information**. Ask yourself "What more can I add?" "What more can I tell them about …?" Be a good guide and a good friend.
☐ **Communicate!**	Be an active listener. React nonverbally to your partner's answers, and comment on them. Ask your partner to explain more, and above all, **communicate**!

Acknowledgements

I'd like to thank Takami Takeuchi and all the members of Hiroshima JALT, for their friendship, support and encouragement over the years. Thanks also to Danny, Lizzy and Alice Haruko Rennie. We wish you many happy returns to Japan!

My sincere thanks to National Geographic Learning and to Tsuyoshi Yoshida in particular, for their faith in this project and for breathing new life into *This Is Japan*.

Simon Capper
The Japanese Red Cross Hiroshima College of Nursing

How to Use This Textbook

This Is Japan will help you to explain a variety of topics related to the Japanese lifestyle and culture. Conversation with foreign friends can sometimes be difficult, but after practicing the topics in this book, you should be ready to start conversations on themes that *you* feel comfortable talking about: "Have you ever eaten Japanese food?" "Do you know much about Japanese manners?" "Have you ever seen Japanese writing?" If your homestay family or new friends aren't familiar with Japanese culture, they'll be happy if you can explain or "teach" them about these topics.

Each unit in *This Is Japan* consists of eight sections:

The **Warm Up** section encourages you to start thinking about the topic and express your thoughts. It's also a good chance to get to know your partner(s), so don't simply answer the questions. Give your partner(s) more information and, if you have time, ask them more questions on the topic.

The **Vocabulary** section introduces the key words that you'll need when you practice with your partner(s). Why not highlight the words that you already know and can use? Then, you can focus on the words that are new to you (and highlight them when you're confident that you know and can use them).

The **Listening** section offers a chance to hear the language used in context. It's not designed to "test" you, so please access the audio and listen to it as many times as you can before class. You will answer the listening comprehension questions about the **Conversation**.

The **Conversation** section offers a chance to practice talking about the topic. Be sure to check your pronunciation, rhythm, stress and intonation with the audio and with your partner.

The **Speaking** section gives you the opportunity to test your communication skills in a safe environment. Practice as much as you can with your partner(s), and when you're in a genuinely intercultural situation, you'll be ready. Don't make the mistake of racing to finish quickly. Always think "What more can I add?" "What more can I tell or ask my partner(s)?" And if you finish the task before your classmates, please keep chatting *in English*!

The **Wrap Up with Danny/Kayla** section works as a reading activity that checks your understanding and provides some more useful vocabulary. This time, it may be a good idea to highlight the words that you *don't* know.

The **Your Turn** section asks you to look outside Japan, do a little research, and get some information and insights about the unit's theme from the perspective of a different culture. After you've prepared "Your Turn" (using the worksheets at the back of the book), be ready to tell your partner(s) about what you've learned.

The **Get Ready** section introduces key vocabulary for the next unit. Try to review these words regularly before starting the new topic. "Meeting" a new word regularly is an important part of learning it. You can see this key vocabulary again in the worksheets at the back of the book. Check (✓) the words you already know and look up any words that you don't know to write their meanings in the blanks.

How to Access the Audio Online

With a smartphone:
1. Scan the QR code on the right to visit the website for the audio.
2. Click a triangle (▶) to play each audio track.

With a computer/PC:
1. Visit the website below.
   https://ngljapan.com/tij-audio/
2. Click a triangle (▶) to play each audio track.

Introduction

Cast of Characters   Who's Who?

Listen to the descriptions of the characters in this book. Fill the gaps with the missing information.

DANNY is a British student spending a year in Japan as part of his B.A. in (1)_____ Studies. He's studying Japanese language and culture. In his free time he enjoys (2)_____, music and traveling. It's his first time in Japan, and he'll stay with the Harada family for three months before moving into student accommodation.

Homestay mother MAKI HARADA lived and worked in Britain as a tour guide. She spent three years there before returning to Japan, getting (3)_____ and starting a family. She now works part-time in the office of an international exchange center. She's a great (4)_____ and is also learning Spanish.

Homestay father YUKIO works for JICA (Japan International Cooperation Agency) and spends long periods of time overseas. He obtained a Master's (5)_____ in the US and now works as an agricultural economist. When he has time, he enjoys playing golf, doing (6)_____ work with an environmental group, and watching documentaries.

Elder sister KUMI is studying international (7)_____ at university. She spent a year studying in Seattle and has also done a homestay in Korea. She is a member of the university lacrosse team. In the future, she's hoping to work for the Red Cross or the (8)_____. She likes Korean music and dramas, and is learning Korean.

Younger brother TAKUYA is a high-school student. He enjoys listening to hip hop music and dancing with his friends. He's a (9)_____ snowboarder and soccer player, and he hopes to talk about soccer with Danny. He enjoys school life, but he's not too keen on (10)_____. He has no idea what he wants to do in the future.

KAYLA is from Seattle. Over the years, her family hosted lots of Japanese students (11)_____ Kumi, and Kayla became curious about visiting Japan. She's now traveling around Japan, and is visiting the Harada family in Hiroshima. She worked for an (12)_____ company in Austin, Texas, but is now between jobs. In her free time, she enjoys running, eating out and watching movies. She's also crazy about rabbits!

Get Ready

Before starting Unit 1, look at this important vocabulary. Go to page 96 for the worksheet.

adjective	anxious	appearance	bald
beard	brother-in-law	definitely	department
describe	gran	grin	heavy-set
idiot	keen (on)	look alike	occupation
outgoing	personality	petite	the black sheep (of the family)

Unit 1

Getting to Know You

Warm Up

Introduce yourself to your partner(s) by answering their questions. Try to give more information about yourself. Then, change roles. Comment on your partner's answers, and try to ask back-up questions. For example:

A: How do you spend your free time?

B: I go shopping, watch YouTube, sometimes go to karaoke with friends.

A: Oh! Who do you follow on YouTube?

B: No one special, just watch make-up stuff, fashion, some music, that kind of thing …

A: Oh, that sounds like me! Do you know …?

Here are some questions your partner(s) will ask you and your possible answers:

1. Where are you from? (Are you from around here?)
   — Yes, I live in ... / No, (I'm not.) I'm from …

2. Do you have any interests? How do you spend your free time?
   — I enjoy _____ing ... / I like _____ing …

3. What's your major?
   — I'm studying ... / I'm in the department of …

4. Have you joined any clubs or circles?
   — Yes, I'm in the ... and the ... / Not yet, but I'm planning to join the …

5. Do you have a part-time job? Are you working anywhere now?
   — Yes, I'm working in a(n) ... / Yes, I work at ...
   — No, not yet (but I'd like to get a job …).

Vocabulary

This vocabulary will help you to describe people. We can talk about their features:

Features	Typical words
character	loud, talkative, quiet, confident
accessories	glasses, earrings, clothes
build or body type	well-built, heavy-set, slim, petite
special features	bearded, bald, tattooed
hair length	short, long, medium-length, shoulder-length
hair style	straight, curly, spiky, wavy
hair color	dark, fair, gray, silver, blonde
face type	round, thin, long, red
smile	friendly, cute, nervous, nice
expression	serious, friendly, nervous, shy, angry, quiet, kind

Work with your partner to match the descriptions (1–8) to the people below.

1. The bald, silver-haired guy with the beard: _____

2. The friendly-looking woman with curly hair and the nice smile: _____

3. The guy with glasses and the friendly smile: _____

4. The young man with the thin face and short dark hair: _____

5. The heavy-set guy with the tattoos: _____

6. The woman who's laughing, with short blonde hair: _____

7. The serious-looking woman with dark, shoulder-length hair: _____

8. The round-faced woman with the beautiful smile: _____

Don

Kristina

Mohammed

Hannah

Aisha

Gus

Ayana

James

Listening

Before You Listen

Before you listen to Danny talking about his family, look at the picture on the next page and discuss the answers to these questions with your partner(s).

1. Which ones do you think are Danny's sisters?

_____

2. How do you think Danny will describe them?

_____

While You Listen

Listen to the conversation and check your answers.

1. Who is the guy with the beard?

_____

2. How did Danny describe himself?

_____

After You Listen

Match each person (1–7) to one of the choices (a–g).

1. Danny's mother

2. Danny's gran

3. Danny's father

4. Danny's younger sister

5. Danny's older sister

6. Danny's older sister's boyfriend

7. Danny's friend

(a) The one in the dark sweater

(b) The one next to Danny's mom

(c) The one who is studying nursing

(d) The one with the big grin

(e) The one who is good at art

(f) The one with the earring

(g) The tall one at the back

Conversation

Danny is telling Maki about his family.

Danny: Maki? Do you want to see some of my family photos?

Maki: Oh, yes please. I've been looking forward to seeing them.

Danny: Here we are then …

Maki: Is that your mom? The one in the dark sweater?

Danny: That's right, and that's my gran next to her. She and her mom look alike, don't they.

Maki: Mmm, they do. And you look like your mother, don't you.

Danny: Yes, I do—in some ways. And that's my dad, the one at the back, next to the door.

Maki: Oh yes, you definitely look more like your mother. Your father's very tall, isn't he.

Danny: Yes, he's taller than me, anyway. The one next to him is my younger sister, Claire. She's really smart, she's studying nursing. And the one on the left is my older sister, Chris. She's the artist of the family. She works for a design company.

Maki: She's very pretty.

Danny: I suppose so, yeah. She's really talkative and outgoing. She's getting married next year. The guy with the beard and the earring is my future brother-in-law, Max.

Maki: So if Chris is the artist of the family, what are you?

Danny: Me? I don't know. Maybe I'm the black sheep of the family!

Maki: I'm sure you're not! Oh! Who's that?! The one with the big grin?

Danny: Oh yeah, that's my friend, Steve. He's an idiot! I've known him since we were kids.

Maki: Your family looks very nice.

Danny: Yeah, they're great. I miss them a lot.

Speaking 1   Getting to Know You

Help each other to get to know class members. Ask your partner(s) about other students in the room. For example:

A: Who's that girl/boy?

B: Which one?

A: The one … (*explain by appearance, clothes, location or actions*)

B: Which one?

A: The one … (*explain again. Give more information*)

B: Oh! That's … S/he … (*give more information*)

We can use the following patterns to identify people:

	with	wearing	in
appearance	The one **with** long hair.		
accessories	The one **with** glasses.	The one **wearing** glasses.	
clothes	The one **with** the red top.	The one **wearing** the red top.	The one **in** the red top.
current actions	The one (who's) talking to John. / The one who's playing with her hair.		
past actions	The one who said "Hi!" / The one who was talking to the teacher.		
location	The one near the door. / The one next to [behind/at the front/etc.] …		

Speaking 2 Talking about Your Family

If you have English-speaking guests or make friends overseas, you might need to talk about your family. Talk with your partner(s) about your family. Try to make extra comments. The examples below will help you.

Ask about occupations: What does your brother [sister/etc.] do?
He works for a construction company. I don't think he enjoys his job very much.
She's a public servant—she works for the prefectural government.

Ask about personality: What's your _____ like?
He's a bit shy, but he's quite friendly when you get to know him.
She's really nice. She has a really good sense of humour and loves ...

Ask about family interests: What does your _____ like doing?
He's crazy about fishing and golf, but he doesn't have much free time.
She loves traveling, so she goes abroad whenever she has a chance.

Wrap Up with Danny

4

Read the passage and answer the questions below.

1 How much do you know about your family history? I'm sure you know about your   01
parents, aunts and uncles, and grandparents. But do you know about your great-grand-   02
parents? Or your great-great-grandparents?!   03
2 The Internet has given us many chances to learn about the world, but in recent years   04
it's also given us the chance to dig back into history and learn about our family history.   05
For example, in Britain, every 10 years, there's a national survey called a census. This   06

census records everyone's personal information (occupation, age, marital status, 07
birthplace, and so on), and all the records from 1841 until 1911 are available online. We 08
can even order copies of our ancestors' birth, marriage and death certificates. 09

3 For this reason, genealogy (the study of family history) has become a really popular 10
hobby. Searching the archive is fascinating, and I've learned a lot about my family 11
history. For example, my great-great grandfather had 12 children! What do you know 12
about your family history? Was your great-great-great grandfather a *samurai*?! 13

1. Which word could best replace the phrase "dig back into history and learn about" in
   Paragraph 2?
   (a) create   (b) research   (c) tell

2. Which of the following sentences is true?
   (a) "Marital status" refers to how long someone has been married.
   (b) "Marital status" refers to if you are married, single, divorced or widowed.
   (c) "Marital status" refers to who is the boss of the house, the husband or the wife.

3. What does "fascinating" in Paragraph 3 mean?
   (a) quite expensive   (b) really interesting   (c) very difficult

Your Turn

Choose one of these activities. Be ready to explain your chosen topic to your partner(s). Go to page
97 for the worksheet.

   (a) What do you know about your family history? Make a family tree.
   (b) Find some old family photos and explain them to your partner(s).

Get Ready

Before starting the next unit, look at this important vocabulary. Go to page 98 for the worksheet.

agriculture	climate	coast	delicacy	dialect
earthquake	historic	hot spring	industry	inland
landslide	natural disaster	prefecture	region	rural
shrine	surrounding area	temple	volcano	weird

Unit 2

My Hometown

Warm Up

Work with your partner(s). Ask and answer the questions about their hometowns. Possible answers are provided. When answering, give additional information. When asking, react and add comments or questions.

1. Where's your favorite place in your hometown?
   — I really like ... / I love going to ...

2. Is there anything you don't like about your hometown?
   — I don't like ... very much. It's ...

3. What's your hometown famous for?
   — Most people know it because ... / It's quite well known for ...

Vocabulary

This vocabulary will help you talk about places in Japan. Complete the sentences below with the words in the box. Use each word only once.

agricultural	earthquakes	hot springs	landslides	prefectures	regions
rainy season	rice fields	shrines	ski resorts	temples	volcanoes

1. There are lots of _____ in Niigata.

2. There are lots of _____ in Kyushu.

3. Small _____ are quite common in Tokyo.

4. Kusatsu (草津) in Gunma Prefecture has some popular _____ .

5. _____ often cause problems in the rainy season.

6. The _____ usually arrives in June.

16

7. There are 47 _____ in Japan.

8. The Tohoku region is a major _____ area.

9. Ise Jingu (伊勢神宮) and Dazaifu Tenmangu (太宰府天満宮) are famous Shinto (神道) _____.

10. Nara is famous for its historic Buddhist _____ .

11. Shiga Kogen (志賀高原) is one of Japan's most popular _____ .

12. Kyushu and Okinawa are the southernmost _____ of Japan.

Listening

Before You Listen

Before you listen to Yukio and Kayla talking about Kayla's adopted hometown, discuss these questions with your partner(s).

1. What do you know about Texas?

_____

2. What kind of food do you imagine is popular there?

_____

While You Listen

Listen to the conversation and answer these questions.

🎧 5

1. How far is Austin from the coast?

_____

2. How does Kayla describe San Antonio?

_____

After You Listen

Tell your partner(s) three things about Austin.

- _____

- _____

- _____

Yukio and Kayla are talking about the city where Kayla lives.

Yukio: So you left home because you got a job in Texas?

Kayla: That's right. In Austin, it's the state capital.

Yukio: So basically, that's down in the southern part of the US, near Mexico?

Kayla: Yeah, Texas is one of the southern states, on the coast, by the Gulf of Mexico. But Austin's quite far inland—it's about a three- or four-hour drive from the coast.

Yukio: What's it famous for?

Kayla: Have you heard of "South by Southwest"? It's an amazing festival, they have it every year in Austin, and so many bands are in town.

Yukio: I've never heard of it. Sounds like fun!

Kayla: Oh, it's fantastic. The city's a big center for the arts and culture. Austin is a bit different from the rest of Texas—they even have a slogan "Keep Austin Weird"!

Yukio: Wow, that *is* weird! I imagine the climate's very dry, like a desert?

Kayla: Not like a desert, but it gets very hot in summer. It's a great place to live, and the food's fantastic too!

Yukio: What kind of food do you have? Any local delicacies?

Kayla: Well, the kind of food you can find all over Texas. There's a lot of Tex-Mex, great barbecues, pecan pie, breakfast tacos—I'm making myself hungry now!

Yukio: Sounds really good! Are there any other famous places near there?

Kayla: Yeah, do you know San Antonio? That's a really nice city, it's very historic too. Have you heard of the Alamo?

Speaking 1   Talking about Your Hometown

If you meet foreign guests or make friends when you're overseas, you may need to talk about your hometown.

Play in groups of three. When it's your turn, play "rock, paper, scissors" with one partner. If you win, move three spaces. If you draw, move two spaces. If you lose, move one space. Your "rock, paper, scissors" partner should ask you the question on the space where you stopped. Answer the question using complete sentences, not single words. Your second partner should ask you back-up questions to show interest and get more information.

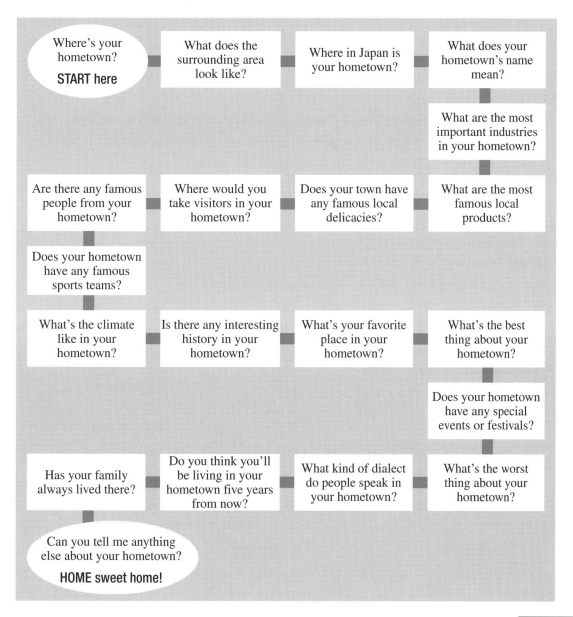

Where's your hometown?

START here

What does the surrounding area look like?

Where in Japan is your hometown?

What does your hometown's name mean?

What are the most important industries in your hometown?

Are there any famous people from your hometown?

Where would you take visitors in your hometown?

Does your town have any famous local delicacies?

What are the most famous local products?

Does your hometown have any famous sports teams?

What's the climate like in your hometown?

Is there any interesting history in your hometown?

What's your favorite place in your hometown?

What's the best thing about your hometown?

Does your hometown have any special events or festivals?

Has your family always lived there?

Do you think you'll be living in your hometown five years from now?

What kind of dialect do people speak in your hometown?

What's the worst thing about your hometown?

Can you tell me anything else about your hometown?

HOME sweet home!

Speaking 2　Why It Is Famous

Ask your partner(s) to tell you about well-known cities in Japan. Then, change roles. Describe their locations, and explain at least three things to see and do there.

Example 1:

Q: Where's Tokyo, and what's it famous for?

A: Tokyo's in the Kanto region. That's the south-east part of Honshu, Japan's main island. It's the capital of Japan, so there are lots of things to see and do. You can go shopping in places like Akihabara and Shinjuku. If you like tall buildings, you can visit Tokyo Tower and Tokyo Skytree. And if you're interested in sumo (相撲), you can see sumo wrestlers in Ryogoku (両国).

Example 2:

Q: Where's Fukuoka, and what's it famous for?

A: Fukuoka is in the northern part of Kyushu, about three hours by bullet train from Osaka. It's famous for *yatai* (屋台). If you go there in the evening, you can see lots of mobile food and drink stands along the city's streets.

Useful expressions to describe a location:

Osaka is on the south coast of central Japan.

Sendai is on the east coast.

Hokkaido is the most northern island.

The Okinawa islands are in the southernmost part of Japan.

Wrap Up with Kayla

Read the passage and answer the questions below.

1 As Yukio already knows, I'm not actually *from* Austin, I just live there. My hometown   01
is Seattle, Washington, in the US northwest. It's quite different from Austin. The climate   02
is very different—people joke that you can get a suntan in Austin, but in Seattle you'll   03
rust! It rains a lot in Seattle, but apart from winter, the weather isn't *so* bad! And Texas   04
often gets droughts when it's dry, and hurricanes, so which is better?   05

2 Seattle is home to some famous companies; Starbucks, Tully's Coffee and Amazon   06
are all based there. Austin doesn't have so many world-famous companies, but it has its   07
famous South by Southwest Festival. Texas also has lower taxes and a lower cost of   08

living, so you can get a bigger house in Austin than in Seattle. That's partly because 09
Texas is four times bigger than Washington—it's also twice the size of Japan! 10
3 The people and their cultures are very different in these states. Texas was part of 11
Mexico until 1836 and nearly 40 percent of the population is Hispanic or Latino. I love 12
that Seattle and Austin are so different. Where will I live in the future? I have no idea, 13
but wherever I am, I hope you can visit! 14

1. According to Paragraph 1, in which conditions is "drought" most likely to happen?
   (a) When hurricanes hit Texas.
   (b) When there isn't enough rain.
   (c) When there is too much rain.

2. What does the phrase "are all based there" in Paragraph 2 mean?
   (a) have offices there
   (b) have their headquarters there
   (c) started their companies there

3. Which of the following sentences is true?
   (a) Kayla prefers life in Seattle to life in Austin.
   (b) Life in Austin is generally cheaper than in Seattle.
   (c) Washington is twice the size of Japan.

Your Turn

Have you ever lived abroad? If you have, get ready to introduce your overseas "hometown" to your partner(s). Talk about its location, popular places, climate, main industries, famous food, sports teams, etc. If you've never lived or stayed overseas for a long period, choose an interesting town or city, research it, and introduce it to your partner(s). Go to page 99 for the worksheet.

Get Ready

Before starting the next unit, look at this important vocabulary. Go to page 100 for the worksheet.

can't stand	crisp(y)	delicacy	disgusting	fermented
fussy eater	ingredients	nutrition	presentation	raw
rubbery	seasonal	seasoning	seaweed	slimy
steam	sticky	stuff	tender	texture

Unit 3

Japanese Food

Warm Up

Work with your partner(s). Ask and answer the questions about food. Possible answers are provided. When answering, give additional information. When asking, react and add comments or questions.

1. What's your favorite Japanese food and why do you like it?
   — I love … / I really like …

2. What's your favorite non-Japanese food and why do you like it?
   — I love … / I really like …

3. What's your least favorite food? Is there any food that you really can't stand?
   — I can't stand … / I really hate …

4. What's the strangest food you've ever eaten?
   — I ate … It was / They were …!

5. What problems might foreign visitors have with Japanese food? Think about people of other religions (Hindus, Jews, Muslims) and other lifestyles (vegetarians and vegans).
   — Maybe they won't like … It's very ... / Some people can't eat … because …

Vocabulary

This vocabulary will help you talk about food. Adjectives are particularly useful to describe texture and taste.

Ⓐ Make sentences with your partner(s) using the words in the box. Note that if you talk about food that is countable, the food in your sentence should be plural. For example:

Potato chips are very crisp.

You do not need to do this if you are using the Japanese name for the food (see the example for Question 1 below).

1. These adjectives of texture are usually negative in English.

chewy	fatty	hard	oily
rubbery	slimy	sticky	

e.g. *Mochi* (餅) are very chewy.

2. These adjectives of texture are usually positive in English.

creamy	crisp(y)	crunchy	firm	fluffy	juicy
light	moist	smooth	soft	spongy	tender

e.g. Kobe beef is usually very tender.

3. These adjectives describe tastes.

bitter	cheesy	chocolaty	fishy
lemony	meaty	nutty	salty
savory	sour	spicy	sweet

e.g. *Anko* (餡子) or red bean paste is very sweet.

4. How the food is prepared is also important.

baked	boiled	deep-fried	dried
fermented	fried	grilled	raw
simmered	smoked	steamed	

e.g. *Hoshigaki* (干し柿) are dried persimmons.

B Which SIX of these words are **not positive** ways to talk about food?

awful	beautiful	bland	brilliant	delicious	disgusting
excellent	fantastic	great	horrible	really good	really nice
superb	tasteless	tasty	wonderful	yucky	yummy

Before You Listen

Before you listen to Maki and Danny talking about food, discuss these questions with your partner(s).

1. Are you a fussy eater?

_____

2. What Japanese food do you think Danny might have trouble with?

_____

While You Listen

Listen to the conversation and answer these questions.

1. How did Danny describe the texture of sea cucumber?

_____

2. Where did Danny first see a sea cucumber?

_____

After You Listen

Tell your partner(s) at least three things that Maki thinks are important when making Japanese lunch boxes.

- _____

- _____

- _____

Conversation

Maki and Danny are eating dinner.

Maki: (*hesitating*) Danny? Are you all right?

Danny: Yes, erm, yeah, I'm, I'm afraid I'm having a bit of trouble with this. It's very (*pause*) chewy and (*swallows*) kind of rubbery.

Maki: What was it? Oh, *namako* (ナマコ)?

Danny: This stuff here. It has a strange texture, doesn't it.

Maki: Have you eaten it before? It's actually a bit of a delicacy.

Danny: No, I don't think so. What's it called?

Maki: In Japanese it's called *namako*. In English, I think it's "sea cucumber."

Danny: Urgh! They look horrible! I've seen them in the aquarium, they're disgusting! Urgh, that's not food! They should just leave them in the sea!

Maki: Oh, it's not that bad! You know, I was a bit worried that you'd be a fussy eater, but you're not difficult at all, are you.

Danny: Oh yeah, I'll try anything. By the way, I really enjoyed that lunch box that you made for me. Thank you—it was fantastic. It must have taken a lot of time to make it.

Maki: Well, thank *you*! I'm glad you liked it. Actually I've been making *bento*s (弁当) for a long time now, so it doesn't take so long. But we still have to think about getting a good balance of ingredients, different textures and tastes, that kind of thing, something boiled, something raw, something fried, and using different seasonings too, like *mirin* (味りん), soy sauce, *miso* ...

Danny: It looked very healthy too.

Maki: Yeah, I try to think about good nutrition, and using seasonal ingredients. And good presentation is important too, choosing the right plates and dishes to make the food look good.

Danny: Well, it's all amazing. I've enjoyed everything you've made for me. Well, apart from that sea cucumber!

Speaking   Japanese Food Bingo

Let's play bingo in pairs. Partner A, go to page 88. Partner B, go to page 92. Follow the instructions:

1. Write the numbers 1–25 AT RANDOM in the grid. Don't show your partner your grid.
2. Your partner will say a number between 1 and 25 (for example,"7").
3. Explain item "7" in your grid, but DON'T SAY THE WORD! Give as much information as you can.
4. When your partner correctly says the word ("Is it ...?"), circle the number on your bingo card.
5. Keep taking turns until both of you have got Bingo!

Example:

A: It's a kind of seaweed. We often use it when we make *miso* soup. It's very healthy.

B: Is it *wakame* (ワカメ)?

A: That's right!

Remember!

· Don't use one-word hints. Use complete sentences.

· Give your partner time to explain.

· Ask questions if you need more information.

These expressions will help you explain things to your partner:

It's a kind of noodle/seaweed/citrus fruit/soft drink.

It's a kind of rice dish/one-pot dish/sushi/root vegetable.

It's a kind of seasoning. We use it with …

It's something we use to ...

It's used in … / We use it in ...

It's long and white, and ...

It's usually eaten ...

We often eat it when we ...

It's made by boiling/drying/grating/steaming.

It's very sticky/sweet/crunchy/chewy.

It's usually made of/from/with/by ...

It's an unusual dish. The *kanji*（漢字）means ...

Shall I tell you how we make it?

Wrap Up with Danny

Read the passage and answer the questions below.

1 The first time I tried *natto*（納豆）, I must admit, I hated it! It was too slimy, too sticky and too smelly—although Maki tells me that these days *natto* doesn't smell as strongly as it used to. And it also tasted pretty bad. But I like to eat strange things, so I practiced a little, and now I can eat it quite happily. It's still not my favorite food, but it's a typical taste of Japan and, I'm told, very healthy.

2 Mmm, delicious! It's strange that in Japan, a country with such a deep and wonderful food culture, there are really only two words for "delicious"—*oishii*（おいしい）and *umai*（うまい）. How strange that Japanese people can enjoy such great food but only use two words to

01
02
03
04
05
06
07
08
09
10
11
12

describe it! And when Japanese use English, they tend to overuse the word "delicious." 13
In English, we have so many other words that we can use to express our feelings—good 14
and bad—about food. How many can you think of? 15

1. Which of these foods has a similar texture to *natto*?
   (a) *chawan mushi*（茶碗蒸し）   **(b)** *tofu*（豆腐）   **(c)** *yamaimo*（山芋）

2. Which of the following sentences is true?
   (a) Danny still can't get used to eating *natto*.
   (b) These days, *natto* has a more powerful smell than in the past.
   (c) When he first ate *natto*, Danny didn't like the texture or the smell.

3. What does Danny think about Japanese speakers of English?
   (a) They have a lot of words to express their feelings about food.
   (b) They talk about food too much.
   (c) They use the word "delicious" too much.

Your Turn

Get ready to introduce three foreign dishes to your partner. Research online to find some tasty and interesting dishes. Do not choose dishes that your partner will certainly know (such as pizza or curry). Be sure to explain the main ingredients and how the dish is made. Go to page 101 for the worksheet.

Get Ready

Before starting the next unit, look at this important vocabulary. Go to page 102 for the worksheet.

altar	draughty	feature	last (a long time)	layout
materials	pillar	prefer	proper	renovate
residential area	scroll	shelf	squat	storage space
straw	suburbs	thatched roof	veranda	woven

Unit 4

The Traditional Japanese House

Warm Up

Work with your partner(s). Ask and answer the questions about housing. Possible answers are provided. When answering, give additional information. When asking, react and add comments or questions.

1. Would you like to live in the house above? Why, or why not?
   — I wouldn't want to live there. I think it might be very cold in winter! And …
   — I'd like to live there. It …

2. What kind of house would you like to live in, Japanese or western-style? Why would you prefer this kind of house?
   — I think I'd rather live in a western-style house. It's probably more comfortable, and ...
   — I'd prefer a(n) …

3. What's your house like? Tell your partner(s) at least four things about your house or apartment. You can talk about its age, location, layout, design, views, etc.
   — We live in a third-floor apartment. It's about 10 years old, and has three bedrooms, a lounge, dining room and kitchen. It's just a normal apartment, but from the balcony we can see some mountains and trees, so it has a nice view. It's in a residential area, in the suburbs, near ...

Vocabulary

This vocabulary will help you talk about houses. Match the photos (1–12) with the phrases below.

____ a Buddhist family altar	____ a pillar	____ an alcove
____ a fireplace	____ a Shinto altar	____ roof tiles
____ a floor plan	____ a thatched roof	____ storage space
____ a hanging scroll	____ a veranda	____ woven straw mats

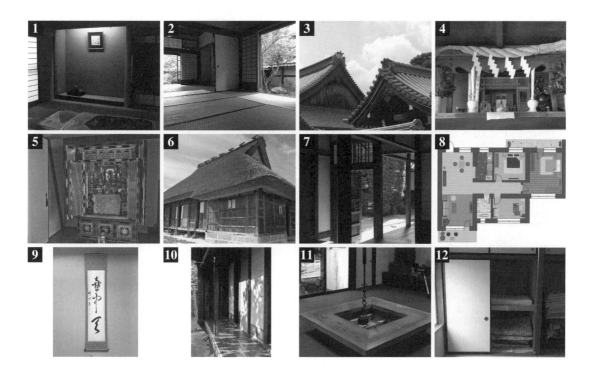

Listening

Before You Listen

Before you listen to Kumi and Kayla talking about traditional houses, discuss these questions with your partner(s).

1. What traditional features of Japanese houses do you like?

2. Have you ever eaten at an *irori* (囲炉裏)?

While You Listen

Listen to the conversation and answer these questions.

1. What separated the main house and the *naya* (納屋)?

2. What kind of house would Kumi prefer to live in?

After You Listen

Answer the questions about the conversation.

1. List three things that have changed since the house was renovated.

   • _____ • _____ • _____

2. What kind of bath did they have in Kumi's grandparents' house?

   _____

Conversation

Kayla is visiting Kumi's grandparents.

Kumi: It's a nice old house, isn't it.

Kayla: Wow! It's amazing! It looks so … so Japanese!

Kumi: My grandparents have lived here a long time, over 50 years.

Kayla: So how old's the house?

Kumi: I'm not sure exactly, but I guess it's over 100 years old.

Kayla: Wow, that's really old for a Japanese house, right?

Kumi: It is. Some parts have been renovated, of course. When I first came here, they still had a *doma* (土間)—that's like an earth-floored area between the main house and a *naya*. The *naya* was where they kept the animals. Now the house has a proper toilet, but when I first came here, they still had a *bottonbenjo* (ぽっとん便所).

Kayla: What's that?

Kumi: It's a toilet, but just a hole. You squat down, and it falls "*botton*" into the hole. You don't see them much these days.

Kayla: Maybe that's not a bad thing!

Kumi: Yeah, they didn't have warm seats or Washlets in those days! They used to have an *irori* too. It's like an open fireplace for cooking. It was nice to sit around the *irori* on a cold winter day! The old houses were usually quite cold and draughty.

Kayla: Would you like to live in a house like this?

Kumi: I like visiting these *noka* (農家)—that's a traditional farmhouse—but I prefer a more modern style. Look, this is the bathroom. They have a normal bath now, but they used to have a *goemonburo* (五右衛門風呂), where you make a fire to heat the water in the bath.

Kayla: Like a big cooking pot?

Kumi: That's right. That's why it's called *goemonburo*. Do you know the story of Ishikawa Goemon?

Kayla: No, I don't …

Speaking   Explaining Traditional Houses

Your English-speaking friends may ask about Japanese houses. Can you explain? With your partner, take turns to explain the items in the pictures below. Partner A, explain the odd numbers (1, 3, 5, 7, 9, etc.). Partner B, explain the even numbers (2, 4, 6, 8, 10, etc.). For example:

A: What's this? *(pointing to number 1)*

B: Ah, let me see. You sometimes see this hanging outside a Japanese home. They're popular in summer ...

■ **Exterior**

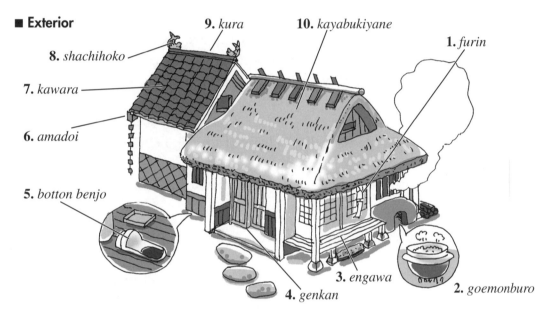

9. *kura*
10. *kayabukiyane*
1. *furin*
8. *shachihoko*
7. *kawara*
6. *amadoi*
5. *botton benjo*
3. *engawa*
4. *genkan*
2. *goemonburo*

■ **Interior**

16. *kakejiku*
17. *oshiire*
18. *butsudan*
19. *ranma*
15. *shoji*
14. *tokonoma*
13. *tatami*
12. *zaisu*
11. *kotatsu*
20. *fusuma*
21. *zabuton*

Wrap Up with Kayla

Read the passage and answer the questions below.

1 When Kumi stayed with my family in Seattle, I can still remember her reaction to 01
seeing our house. Of course, it was bigger than her home in Japan. American homes are, 02
on average, twice the size of Japanese homes. But it wasn't just the size that surprised 03
her. There were many other differences, for example, our house has a basement and an 04
attic. Japanese homes don't have basements, and almost never have attics. 05

2 Our house is nearly 100 years old. That's pretty old by American standards, and very 06
old for Japanese. But my British friend tells me that in Britain, a 100-year-old house is 07
not particularly old. Houses there last longer because they're usually built of brick or 08
stone—Brits don't have to worry about earthquakes. In Seattle, we do, so houses are 09
usually wooden or concrete-built. Brits also have a strong sense of history, so older 10
buildings are usually more popular than new ones—quite the opposite of Japan! 11

3 Finally, in Britain and the States, the geology, history and climate are much more 12
varied. The type of local stone, the purpose of the house and the period that it was built 13
in, all influence house design, so there are much greater differences in housing style 14
than in Japan. 15

1. Which of the following best completes the sentence below?

   An attic is a room found _____ of a house.

   (a) at the back   **(b)** at the top   **(c)** below the ground floor

2. Complete the sentence below with a suitable word from Paragraph 2.

   As in Japan, builders in Seattle need to build houses that can survive

   _____.

3. Which of the following sentences is true?
   (a) House styles in the US and Britain are as varied as in Japan.
   (b) House styles in the US and Britain are less varied than in Japan.
   (c) House styles in the US and Britain are more varied than in Japan.

Your Turn

Choose one of these activities. Be ready to explain your chosen topic to your partner(s). Go to page 103 for the worksheet.

   (a) Think about your dream house. What would it look like? What special features would you like it to have? Make notes and be ready to explain your dream house to your partner(s).

   (b) Research four differences between Japanese-style houses and western-style houses. Be ready to explain them to your partner(s).

Get Ready

Before starting the next unit, look at this important vocabulary. Go to page 104 for the worksheet.

adjective	adverb	bother	character	combination
consonant	flea	look something up	memorize	noun
particle	phonetic	pronunciation	rhythm	stress
stroke order	syllable	verb	vowel	word ending

Unit 5

The Japanese Language

Warm Up

A Write your name and explain it to your partner in English. Then, ask about your partner's name. For example:

A: My name's Aiko Tasaka, but most of my friends call me *Ai-chan*. *Ai* (愛) means "love" and *ko* (子) means "child." *Ta* (田) means "rice field" and *saka* (坂) means "slope" or "hill."

B: Do you like your name? Why did your parents call you _____?

B Work with your partner(s). Ask and answer the questions about learning Japanese and learning English. Possible answers are provided. When answering, give additional information. When asking, react and add comments or questions.

1. What do you think would be difficult for foreigners learning Japanese? Say three things and write a "key word" for each of them.
   — I think memorizing so many characters must be very difficult.   [memorizing]

   _____   _____   _____

2. What do you think causes most problems for Japanese learning English? Say three things and write a "key word" for each of them.
   — Pronunciation is really difficult. Some English sounds aren't in Japanese.   [pronunciation]

   _____   _____   _____

Vocabulary

This vocabulary will help you talk about the Japanese language. Complete the sentences below with the words in the box. Use each word only once.

adjective	characters	foreign	expressing	originally
particles	phonetic	readings	surnames	syllable

1. *Katakana* (カタカナ) is mostly used for writing _____ names and words.

2. *Hiragana* (ひらがな) is often used for writing _____, such as *wa*, *ni*, *wo* and *mo*.

3. *Furigana* (ふりがな) is used for making difficult _____ easier to read.

4. Each *katakana* and *hiragana* symbol is a unique _____.

5. Verb and _____ endings are usually written using *okurigana* (送り仮名).

6. *Katakana* is sometimes used to write words _____ sounds, such as *zaazaa* (ザ アザア) and *gorogoro* (ゴロゴロ).

7. *Hiragana* and *katakana* are used like _____ symbols.

8. *Kanji* _____ came to Japan from China around 2,000 years ago.

9. Most Japanese _____ are written using *kanji*.

10. *Hiragana* and *katakana* only represent sounds, but *kanji* may have many different meanings and _____.

Listening

Before You Listen

Before you listen to Danny and Maki talking about the Japanese language, discuss the question below with your partner(s).

Do you understand how to count syllables in English? How many syllables are there in these words?

black ____   language ____   practical ____   sprinkle ____   stand ____

While You Listen

Listen to the conversation and answer these questions.

1. Which two English words does Danny say sound the same in *katakana*?

_____

2. How does Maki explain *dani* (ダニ) to Danny?

_____

After You Listen

Answer these questions about the conversation.

1. Why is *katakana* useful for Japanese?

_____

2. How can you sound more natural in English?

_____

Conversation

Danny and Maki are talking about the Japanese language.

Danny: So, *katakana*'s mostly used for writing foreign words?

Maki: Yeah, it's really useful for bringing foreign words into Japanese, but that's not good for our English pronunciation. There are quite a few sounds in English that we don't have in Japanese.

Danny: Like "v," and "f" and "r/l" sounds? And having no "th" like in "thin" or "si" like in "sit"? And Japanese only has five vowel sounds too, right, so "bus" and "bath" sound the same to you—and "earth" sounds very different in *katakana*!

Maki: Yeah, the sounds of English are different, and in *katakana*, almost every sound is a consonant and vowel combination, so the rhythm of Japanese is very different too.

Danny: How do you mean? Can you give me an example?

Maki: OK, so if you have a name like McDonald—in English it only has three syllables, but in Japanese, it has six—*Ma-ku-do-na-ru-do*! That really messes up the rhythm. It doesn't sound very English, does it.

Danny: Yeah, I see what you mean. It sounds a bit funny when you say it in *katakana*. When you put an English word into *katakana*, it really isn't English any more—it's Japanese!

Maki: Right. So to sound natural in English, we have to listen to it a lot, and really feel the stress and rhythm.

Danny: Talking of names, Takuya was joking about my name today.

Maki: Well, you know what *dani* means, don't you? It's a kind of insect. What do you call them? Oh, a bit like a "flea," you know, like in "flea market"?

Danny: Flea?! Oh no! That's terrible!

Maki: Oh, it's kind of cute really. Don't let it bother you!

Danny: What's the *kanji* for *dani*?

Maki: Oooh, hold on, I'll have to look it up …

Speaking 1   Explaining *Kanji*

People who aren't familiar with *kanji* are usually interested in learning about them. Explain the *kanji* below to your partner(s). Here are some examples:

堀   This character's parts are "earth," "door" and "exit," and together they mean "moat."

温   This character means "warm." This part means "water," this part means "sun," and this part means "dish" or "plate." If the sun shines on a dish of water, it becomes warm.

茶色   This combination of "tea" and "color" means "brown."

家内   This is a combination of "house" and "inside." Together they mean "wife."

森	靴	薬	鮃	鯖	鰯	鳴く	町
秋	鰈	花	晴	峠	蝶	噛む	砂
鉛筆	電車	朝顔	休館日	馬車	花火	競馬場	向日葵
兄弟	眼鏡	自動車	教室	黒子	金魚	体温計	火山

Speaking 2   Explaining Japanese Writing

The Japanese writing systems—*kanji*, *hiragana* and *katakana*—are difficult for many non-Japanese to understand. Explain the different writing systems to your partner(s). Ask and answer the questions. When answering, use the key points and give additional information or examples.

Questions	Key Points
Kanji	
Tell me about *kanji*. Where did they come from?	Explain *kanji* history (*kan* = China / 2,000 years ago)
How many *kanji* do you have to learn?	Explain 1,026 *kyoiku* (教育) *kanji* / 2,136 *joyo* (常用) *kanji*
What do you use *kanji* for?	Explain use in nouns, verbs, adjectives, etc.
Is it true that *kanji* are like pictures?	Explain some *kanji* origins.
Does each *kanji* have only one pronunciation?	Explain *kunyomi*—the way a *kanji* is pronounced by itself, and *onyomi*—the way *kanji* are pronounced in combinations.
What are the parts of a *kanji*?	Explain *bushu* (部首).

Questions	Key Points
Hiragana	
Tell me about *hiragana*. What do you use them for?	Explain making difficult *kanji* easier to read (*furigana* in children's books); use in verb, adverb and adjective endings (*okurigana*) and prepositions.
How were *hiragana* made?	Explain about simplified versions of *kanji*.
When were *hiragana* made?	Explain 1,000 years ago, Heian period.
Katakana	
Tell me about *katakana*. What do you use them for?	Explain use in foreign names and foreign words. Also in sounds and "impact" words.
How were *katakana* made?	Explain how *katakana* were made from parts of *kanji*.
When were *katakana* made?	Explain *katakana* history, 1,000 years ago, Heian period.

Wrap Up with Danny 🎧 12

Read the passage and answer the questions below.

1 When I was younger, I couldn't imagine coming to Japan or learning Japanese, but   01
since I arrived here and since I started my course, I've been really excited to try to speak   02
Japanese fluently. It's a challenge. Japanese is much harder than English—and learning   03
to read in Japanese can be a real barrier—but this is a marathon, not a sprint!   04

2 Now that I've felt the excitement of being   05
able to communicate in a foreign language, I   06
feel a little sad that most of my friends haven't   07
had the same experience. Not many British   08
people learn a second language. Maybe they   09
were discouraged by too many tests, and not   10
having the chance to actually use the   11
language, but I want to tell them that speaking   12
a second language is a wonderful thing. It   13
opens a door, like a magic key—a door to new   14
ways of thinking, new experiences and   15
opportunities, to new friends.   16

3 To be honest, I don't know if I'll use   17

38

Japanese in the future or not. I have no idea what career path I'm going to follow. But   18
how exciting it will be if, when I'm back in England, I can meet Japanese people and   19
communicate with them.   20

1. Which of the following sentences is true?
    (a) Danny always dreamed of coming to Japan and learning the language.
    (b) Danny knows it will take a long time to become fluent in Japanese.
    (c) Danny suggests that speaking is harder than reading Japanese.

2. What does the word "discouraged" in Paragraph 2 mean?
    (a) to become tired and lack energy
    (b) to have a strong desire to get a good result
    (c) to have lost confidence or enthusiasm

3. Which of the following sentences is true?
    (a) Danny doesn't think he will use Japanese much after he leaves Japan.
    (b) Danny isn't sure what kind of job he will do in the future.
    (c) When he is in England, Danny is going to find a job where he needs to speak
        Japanese.

Your Turn

Learn about a writing system from another culture. Make sure you can understand the sounds and be ready to explain it to your partner(s). It's easier if you use a chart or an illustration. Go to page 105 for the worksheet.

Get Ready

Before starting the next unit, look at this important vocabulary. Go to page 106 for the worksheet.

beckon	calligraphy	cheap	customer	earwax
expensive	fan	fold	lacquer	lantern
light	pack	paw	scoop	souvenir
suitable	sword	traditional	weapon	wrap

Unit 6

Explaining Japanese Things

Warm Up

Imagine you are going to do a homestay in a foreign country. Ask your partner(s) these questions about the Japanese souvenirs that they would choose for their host family. Then, change roles. When answering, give reasons for your choices.

1. What Japanese souvenirs would be good for a mother or father?

2. What would be good for a young girl or boy?

3. What gifts would be good for teenagers?

4. What would be good for an older woman or man?

Some example responses:
· If there was a teenage boy, I'd probably give him …
· Most older people seem to like …, so I'd probably take …
· My grandmother really likes …, so an older woman might like ...
· I don't think a *furoshiki* (風呂敷) would be suitable for a teenage boy!
· … would be good for a host mother.
· … is/are always popular.

Vocabulary

This vocabulary will help you talk about typical gifts and other things that are not familiar to many non-Japanese. Match the photos (1–16) of popular souvenirs with the correct English words below. When you finish, check your answers with your partner(s). For example:

A: What do you think this is?
B: I think it's a calligraphy brush.
A: Yeah, I think so too.

____ ball and cup game

____ beckoning cat

____ calligraphy brush

____ devil mask

____ earwax scraper

____ flower stand

____ folding fan

____ headband

____ lacquer bowl

____ paper lantern

____ personal seal

____ rice scoop

____ sword

____ good-luck doll

____ wind chime

____ wrapping cloth

Listening

Before You Listen

Before you listen to Kayla and Takuya talking about Kayla's souvenirs, discuss these questions with your partner(s):

1. What's the best souvenir that you've ever received?

_____

2. Which of the souvenirs on this page would you most like to receive?

_____

While You Listen

Listen to the conversation and answer these questions.

1. How did Takuya misunderstand Kayla's comment about the cat's hand?

_____

2. Why did Kayla buy so many folding fans?

_____

After You Listen

Go back to the photos on page 41 and circle the seven souvenirs that Kayla bought.

Conversation

🎧 13 🎧

Kayla is showing Takuya the souvenirs that she bought.

Kayla: Look, I got some souvenirs to take home.

Takuya: Oh! You got one of these! You see its hand?

Kayla: *(interrupting)* Its paw?

Takuya: No, it's not poor. It has money! This is a *koban* (小判), it's an old Japanese gold coin.

Kayla: No, we call a cat's hand a paw.

Takuya: Oh, OK, poor cat … *kawaiso* (かわいそう) … this is "*neko ni koban* (猫に小判)," it's a waste of money to give it to a cat. This hand up means he wants friends, and if he raises the other hand, he's inviting customers.

Kayla: I see. And this? Is it a *ninja* (忍者) weapon?

Takuya: No, no it isn't! *(laughs)* It's not for *ninja*, it's for *ikebana* (生け花), for flower arranging! We stick them on, like this.

Kayla: Oh—right!

42

Takuya: Right, it's not a *ninja shuriken* (手裏剣). It's called a *kenzan* (剣山).

Kayla: And this?

Takuya: This is to make your dreams come true. You paint one eye here, make a wish, then paint the other eye when the wish comes true.

Kayla: Oh great. What would you wish for?

Takuya: A nice girlfriend!

Kayla: *(laughs)* And this? What does it say?

Takuya: Oh, it's a headband, it says you'll "definitely win!"

Kayla: Great! We will win!

Takuya: Definitely! Oh, you got fans too.

Kayla: Yeah, I got loads of these folding fans—they're light and cheap, and I got these wind chimes too.

Takuya: Wind chimes, oh right … yeah, these are really popular in summer.

Kayla: Yeah, I got four of those. And this ball and cup game. What's it called in Japanese?

Speaking   Japanese Things Bingo

Let's play bingo in pairs. Partner A, go to page 89. Partner B, go to page 93. Follow the instructions:

1. Write the numbers 1–25 AT RANDOM in the grid. Don't show your partner your grid.
2. Your partner will say a number between 1 and 25 (for example "7").
3. Explain item "7" in your grid, but DON'T SAY THE WORD! Give as much information as you can.
4. When your partner correctly says the word ("Is it …?"), circle the number on your bingo card.
5. Keep taking turns until both of you have got Bingo!

Example 1:

A: It's a kind of envelope that we use for giving gifts of money. The decoration is very pretty and colorful, and it has a bow on it to tie up the happiness of the couple.

B: Is it a *shugibukuro* (祝儀袋)?

A: That's right!

Example 2:

A: It's something we wear in summer when we go to a festival or to watch fireworks. It's a kind of colorful, light kimono.

B: Is it a *yukata* (浴衣)?

A: Yes, well done!

Remember!

· Don't use one-word hints. Use complete sentences.

· Give your partner time to explain.

· Ask questions if you need more information.

These expressions will help you explain things to your partner:

It's a kind of ...

It's like a(n) ...

It's usually made of/from ...

It's something we use to (sign important documents and papers).

It's something we send to (wish someone a happy summer).

It's something we wear when we (go to a festival or summer fireworks).

It's something we eat when we (celebrate the new year).

Wrap Up with Kayla

🎧 14

Read the passage and answer the questions below.

1 *Samue* (作務衣), *jimbei* (甚平), *hanten* (半纏), *happi* (法被) and *chanchanko* (ちゃんちゃんこ)? 01
When are these usually worn? *Hakama* (袴), kimono, *yukata* and *nemaki* (寝巻)? *Geta* (下駄), 02
waraji (草鞋), *jikatabi* (地下足袋) and *zori* (草履)? Can you explain the differences? 03

2 Japan seems to have dress codes for every situation and every activity. Formal suits 04
for weddings and funerals can't just be black, they have to be *black* black! Take your 05
shoes off in the house, but put slippers on when you visit a school—and change to toilet 06
slippers when you go to the bathroom. In the US, we don't keep changing our shoes, and 07
we usually wear them in the house. 08

3 In Japan, you use a special 09
envelope for a new-year gift, a 10
decorative envelope for a 11
wedding—and of course, it's 12
not the same envelope as you 13
use for a donation at a 14
funeral. In the US, we don't 15
usually give gifts of money, 16
but when we do, we don't use 17
a special envelope. No frills, 18
no fuss! 19

4 Life is simpler in the US, but that's what makes Japan so interesting. Learning these 21
social rules can be confusing, but it's worth it. Japan is a charming and fascinating place 21
to visit. Now, am I wearing a *yukata*? Or is it a *happi*? 22

1. Which of the following does Kayla not mention?
   (a) *koden*（香典）　　(b) *nengajo*（年賀状）　　(c) *otoshidama*（お年玉）

2. What does the expression "No frills, no fuss!" in Paragraph 3 mean?
   (a) Don't give someone a gift of money.
   (b) Keep things simple.
   (c) Prepare things carefully.

3. How does Kayla feel about the social rules in Japan?
   (a) They're quite complicated.
   (b) They're quite easy to follow.
   (c) They're too strict.

Your Turn

Kayla talked about the very formal clothes that are needed for Japanese weddings and funerals. What about other cultures and other religions? Research wedding and funeral customs from another culture. Write four points for each ceremony. Be ready to explain them to your partner(s). Go to page 107 for the worksheet.

Get Ready

Before starting the next unit, look at this important vocabulary. Go to page 108 for the worksheet.

accidentally	appropriate	avoid	complain	complicated
confusing	decorative	drag	funeral	grave
habit	incense	lick	on purpose	permission
spear	stab	superstition	table manners	tear

Review Game Units 1–6

Play in groups of three. When it's your turn, play "rock, paper, scissors" with one partner. If you win, move three spaces. If you draw, move two spaces. If you lose, move one space.

Your "rock, paper, scissors" partner should ask you the question on the space where you stopped. Answer the question using complete sentences, not single words. Your second partner should ask you back-up questions to show interest and get more information.

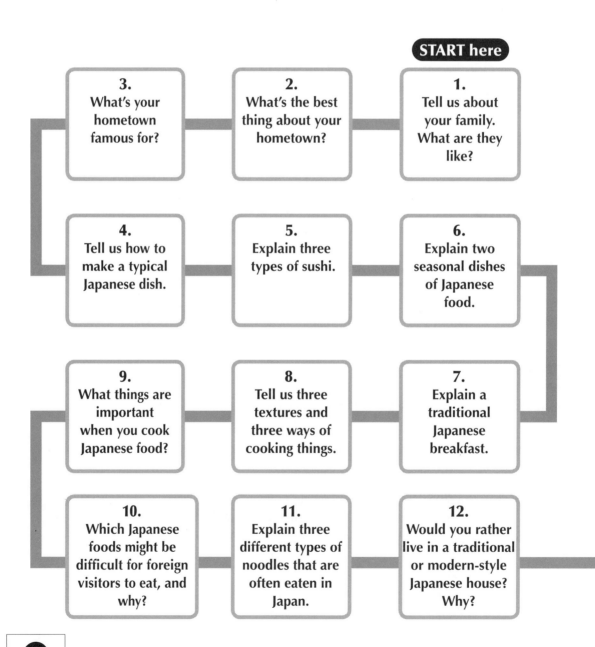

START here

3.
What's your hometown famous for?

2.
What's the best thing about your hometown?

1.
Tell us about your family. What are they like?

4.
Tell us how to make a typical Japanese dish.

5.
Explain three types of sushi.

6.
Explain two seasonal dishes of Japanese food.

9.
What things are important when you cook Japanese food?

8.
Tell us three textures and three ways of cooking things.

7.
Explain a traditional Japanese breakfast.

10.
Which Japanese foods might be difficult for foreign visitors to eat, and why?

11.
Explain three different types of noodles that are often eaten in Japan.

12.
Would you rather live in a traditional or modern-style Japanese house? Why?

GOAL

30.
Explain how people use *sento*（銭湯）.

29.
Explain *nengajo*.

28.
What's a *kappa*（合羽）?

25.
How and when do you use *inkan* (*hanko*).

26.
When and why do people fly *koinobori*（鯉のぼり）?

27.
Why does the *manekineko*（招き猫）have its paw raised?

24.
Explain *hamaya* and *kadomatsu*（門松）.

23.
Name and explain three types of Japanese footwear.

22.
Name and explain three types of Japanese clothing.

19.
Explain *onyomi* and *kunyomi*, giving examples.

20.
How is English difficult for Japanese learners?

21.
What does *banzai*（万歳）mean, and why do people do it?

18.
What are *kanji* used for?

17.
What is *hiragana* used for?

16.
What is *katakana* used for?

13.
Explain three features found in a traditional Japanese-style house.

14.
Tell us four things about your house.

15.
Tell us the story of Ishikawa Goemon.

Unit 7

Good Manners, Bad Manners

Warm Up

Discuss these pictures with your partner(s) and complete the sentences.

 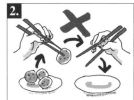  

1. He shouldn't _____.

2. It's bad manners to _____.

3. It's not good to _____.

4. It's not polite to _____.

Vocabulary

This vocabulary will help you talk about etiquette and manners. Complete the sentences below with the words in the box. Use each word only once.

appropriate	avoid	bowing	complicated	envelope
formal	incense	receive	superstitious	unwrap

1. In very _____ situations we need to be more polite.

2. It's bad manners to blow out burning _____ with your breath.

3. A gift of money is usually given in a special decorative _____.

4. If you visit someone's house, you should take a(n) _____ gift.

5. The rules for exchanging business cards aren't so _____.

6. Try to _____ walking between people when they are talking.

7. It's polite to _____ gifts carefully, without tearing the paper.

8. You should _____ someone's business card with both hands.

9. _____ is a common way of greeting someone in Japan.

10. Some people are very _____ about the numbers 4 and 9.

Listening

Before You Listen

Before you listen to Danny and Kumi talking about manners, discuss these questions with your partner(s).

1. What are five things you shouldn't do with chopsticks?

_____

2. What do you think are bad table manners?

_____

While You Listen

🎧 15 🎧

Listen to the conversation and answer these questions.

1. Why don't people pass food to each other using chopsticks?

_____

2. What three things did Takuya's mother tell him to do?

_____

After You Listen

Kumi told Danny eight things *not to do* with chopsticks. List five of them using key words.

- _____

- _____

- _____

- _____

- _____

Danny is having dinner with the Harada family.

Danny: Sorry, Kumi, what was all that about?

Kumi: Oh, don't worry, mom was complaining about Takuya's table manners.

Danny: Like what? What was he doing?

Kumi: She was telling him not to use just one chopstick by itself, and to sit up straight.

Danny: Why can't he use one chopstick?

Kumi: I don't know. It's just bad manners, I suppose.

Danny: So what else is bad manners? I mean, using chopsticks isn't difficult, but are there things I shouldn't do?

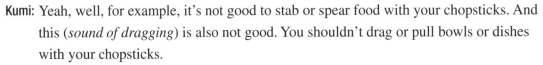

Kumi: Yeah, well, for example, it's not good to stab or spear food with your chopsticks. And this *(sound of dragging)* is also not good. You shouldn't drag or pull bowls or dishes with your chopsticks.

Danny: Oh, like this? *(sound of long dragging)* I didn't know that!

Kumi: Yeah, just like that! *(sound of more dragging)* OK, Danny, stop it!

Danny: Someone told me I should never, ever pass food from chopsticks to chopsticks.

Kumi: That's right. That's a real no-no. It's something to do with funerals. And so is standing your chopsticks up in rice.

Danny: You mean like this?

Kumi: No! Danny! I'm not joking! Don't do it!

Danny: I never realized it was so complicated.

Kumi: It's best to watch other people and try to copy them. Oh, and I just remembered something else. It's not good to point at things with your chopsticks, or lick them.

Danny: OK, no pointing and no licking!

Kumi: And you shouldn't do what Takuya's doing now! He's using his chopsticks to look for the best bits of food on the plate! Stop it Takuya!

Takuya: *Ii jan* (いいじゃん)!

Maki: Takuya! *Yamenasai* (やめなさい)!

Speaking 1   Talking about the "Rules" of Japanese Etiquette

Discuss the situations (1–6) with your partner(s). Identify three "rules" for each situation and practice giving advice to foreign visitors. Write key words to show each piece of advice.

These expressions will help you:

<u>It's better to</u> turn your business card round to face the other person.

<u>Try to avoid</u> getting any soap or shampoo in the bathwater.

<u>Don't / Never</u> use a *shugibukuro* wedding envelope for funeral *koden.* *

<u>Try not to</u> look disappointed even if you don't like a gift.

<u>You should</u> wash your hands before you enter a shrine.

<u>You have to</u> take your shoes off in the *genkan*（玄関）.**

*This form is used when you give very strong advice.

**This form is used when you have no choice.

1. Exchanging business cards

Key words:

_____

_____

_____

2. Taking a bath in a hot spring

Key words:

_____

_____

_____

3. Attending a wedding or a funeral

Key words:

_____

_____

_____

4. Giving and receiving gifts

Key words:

_____

_____

_____

5. Visiting a shrine or temple

Key words:

_____

_____

_____

6. Visiting someone's house

Key words:

_____

_____

_____

Speaking 2   The Do's and Don'ts Quiz

A   Look at the pictures below and tell your partner the key words. Can your partner give you some good advice? For example:

A: wait / *kampai* （乾杯）！

B: If you go to a party, you have to wait for the *kampai* before you start drinking.

B   Now ask your partner about the reasons for the manners in the pictures above. For example:

A: Why do we have to take our shoes off in the house?

B: Shoes are often dirty, and they can damage *tatami* （畳）.

Wrap Up with Danny

Read the passage and answer the questions below.

1   When I first came to Japan, there seemed to be so many rules of social etiquette.   01
People here always seemed so careful and polite. I was always worried about making   02
mistakes. I didn't want people to see me as a big, clumsy foreigner! But my Japanese   03
friends were very understanding, and they knew that most of my mistakes were not on   04
purpose.   05

2 Sometimes though, it wasn't bad manners, I just made mistakes because I didn't 06
know anything about superstitions. Once I gave a friend a potted plant when I visited 07
her in hospital. I didn't know that this was bad luck. Luckily, she got better! I also gave a 08
set of kitchen knives to some friends as a wedding present. Sadly they got divorced a 09
year later, but it wasn't my fault! For a long time I slept with my pillow pointing north, 10
until my friends explained why I shouldn't. The same friends told me that I shouldn't 11
write people's names using a red pen. Is that true? Why shouldn't we do these things? 12
3 To be honest, I'm not at all superstitious. And as for palm reading, horoscopes, and 13
blood types—I really don't believe that nonsense! Do you? 14

1. What is the opposite of "on purpose" in Paragraph 1?
   (a) as usual   **(b)** by accident   **(c)** of course

2. Which of the following sentences is true?
   (a) Danny believes that certain things will cause bad luck.
   (b) Danny caused his friends divorce.
   (c) Despite Danny's "unlucky" gift, his hospitalized friend recovered.

3. Which superstition did Danny NOT mention?
   (a) *hoshiuranai* （星占い）
   (b) *teruterubozu* （てるてる坊主）
   (c) *tesouranai* （手相占い）

Your Turn

Research and make notes about three examples of good or bad manners from non-Japanese cultures. Be ready to explain them to your partner(s). Go to page 109 for the worksheet.

Get Ready

Before starting the next unit, look at this important vocabulary. Go to page 110 for the worksheet.

according to …	ancestor	branch	ceremony	coming of age
commemorate	constitution	custom	decorate	display
equinox	fireworks	foundation	labor	legend
lunar	purify	ritual	wild boar	zodiac

Unit 8

Special Days and Events

Warm Up

Work with your partner(s). Ask and answer the questions about special days and events. Possible answers are provided. When answering, give additional information. When asking, react and add comments or questions.

1. What's your favorite festival or holiday? Why do you like it?
    — My favorite is ... I really enjoy ... / Our local festival is ...

2. Is the New Year important to you? Why, or why not?
    — For me, New Year is really special. It's a great time to ...

3. Can you tell the story behind *tanabata* （七夕）or explain *obon* （お盆）?
    — It's a story about two lovers, Orihime （織姫）and Hikoboshi （彦星）. They ...

Vocabulary

This vocabulary will help you talk about special days and events. Complete the sentences below with the words in the box. Use each word only once.

ancestors	ceremony	commemorate	custom	funeral
lanterns	legend	lunar	purify	ritual

1. A *dampatsushiki* （断髪式）is a hair-cutting _____ for a retiring sumo wrestler.

2. According to _____ , Orihime and Hikoboshi meet only once a year.

3. Bowing is part of the _____ before praying at a shrine.

4. Every year at *obon* we pray to our _____ .

5. In some parts of Japan, graves are decorated with paper _____ at *obon*.

6. It's important to wear appropriate clothes at a _____ .

7. *Kisaragi* (如月) and *kannazuki* (神無月) are months in the old _____ calendar.

8. Throwing dried beans at the devil is a popular _____ at *setsubun* (節分).

9. We _____ the atomic bombing of Hiroshima and Nagasaki every August.

10. We wash our hands to _____ ourselves before praying at a shrine.

Listening

Before You Listen

Before you listen to Kayla and Kumi talking about *tanabata* and *obon*, discuss the answers to these questions with your partner(s).

1. What two things are usually displayed at *tanabata*?

_____

2. What do people usually do at *obon*?

_____

While You Listen

Listen to the conversation and answer these questions.

🎧 17

1. What does Kayla call the *Amanogawa* (天の川)?

_____

2. Why does Kumi like *obon* more than Halloween?

_____

After You Listen

What four fun things did Kumi talk about doing at *obon*?

- _____

- _____

- _____

- _____

Kayla is asking Kumi about some festivals.

Kayla: Some people in the mall asked me to write a wish on a piece of paper and they tied it to a branch of bamboo. What were they doing?

Kumi: Ahhh, that's *tanabata*.

Kayla: Oh, right, good, uhm, what exactly is *tanabata*? They couldn't explain it.

Kumi: *Tanabata*? It's a festival we have every year on July 7th. According to legend, there are two stars that are lovers, but they can only meet once a year, by crossing the … uhmm … what do you call it? It's like a big river of stars in the sky.

Kayla: Oh, the Milky Way?

Kumi: Yeah, that's it. The two lovers, Orihime and Hikoboshi, can cross the Milky Way once a year on the seventh day of the seventh month. I think it came from China. Anyway, we write a wish on a piece of paper, and tie it to the bamboo. It's really big in Sendai, and in some places *tanabata* is connected to *obon*.

Kayla: And *obon* is …?

Kumi: It's a Buddhist festival in summer. It's when the spirits of our ancestors return home to visit us. We usually get a short holiday so we can go home to clean up the family graves. And we pray to the ancestors, burn incense, leave some flowers, that kind of thing.

Kayla: It sounds a bit like Halloween. That started as a festival for the dead.

Kumi: Yeah, I think I prefer *obon* though. It's not so scary! We can meet our friends, go to a *bon-odori* (盆踊り)—that's a kind of dance—and wear a *yukata*—you know, the light summer kimono—and watch a fireworks display too. It's great!

Kayla: Sounds fun.

Speaking 1   Celebrating New Year in Japan

It's easy to explain *onsen* as "It's a hot bath." But this really doesn't explain the concept of *onsen* in the way that Japanese people understand and experience them. *Onsen* bathing in Japan is associated with:

- · health benefits
- · social communication
- · tourism
- · relaxation
- · the bathing "ritual"

In short, it's much more than "a hot bath," and you need to explain that.

In the US and UK, New Year is associated with:

- · New Year resolutions
- · kissing, hugging, and greetings
- · shop sales
- · drinking parties and the countdown (10-9-8-7-6…)

What associations does New Year have in Japan? With your partner(s), list 12 things that are associated with celebrating the New Year in Japan. Then, take turns explaining them to your partner(s). For example:

A: What's a *hamaya* (破魔矢)?

B: It's a decorative arrow. We can get one from a shrine when we do a New Year visit. It's supposed to bring good luck for the year, or keep bad luck away.

Speaking 2   Special Days and Events Bingo

Let's play bingo in pairs. Partner A, go to page 90. Partner B, go to page 94. Follow the instructions:

1. Write the numbers 1–25 AT RANDOM in the grid. Don't show your partner your grid.
2. Your partner will say a number between 1 and 25 (for example "7").
3. Explain item "7" in your grid, but DON'T SAY THE WORD! Give as much information as you can.
4. When your partner correctly says the word ("Is it …?"), circle the number on your bingo card.
5. Keep taking turns until both of you have got Bingo!

Example 1:

A: It's a public holiday at the end of April. It was the birthday of the Showa Emperor. We don't do anything special. It used to be called Greenery Day, but that's on May 4th now.

B: That's an easy one. I think it's *Showa no hi*.

A: That's right.

Example 2:

A: It's a sumo purification ritual. When the sumo wrestler enters the *dohyo* (土俵), he lifts his leg up and stamps down on the ground to scare away bad spirits. Finally, he throws salt to purify the ring.

B: Oh, is that called *shiko* (四股)?

A: It is! Well done, I didn't think you'd get that one.

Remember!

· Don't use one-word hints. Use complete sentences.
· Give your partner time to explain.
· Ask questions if you need more information.

These expressions will help you explain things to your partner:

It's a time when ...	It's a ritual for/to ...
It's a ceremony where/when/to ...	It's a (special) day when ...
It's a tradition when/where ...	It's a day to commemorate ...
It's a party where/for ...	It's a festival where ...
It's a custom where ...	We usually ...

Wrap Up with Kayla

🎧 18

Read the passage and answer the questions below.

1 In the US, New Year isn't such a big deal. For us, Thanksgiving and Christmas are   01
more important celebrations. In most parts of Britain too, New Year isn't so important,   02
but my grandparents were Scottish, and in Scotland, New Year is very important indeed.   03

2 In Scotland, New Year is known as   04
Hogmanay, and there are lots of customs that   05
are unique to this nation. Perhaps the most   06
famous is the singing of a song called "Auld   07
Lang Syne." At midnight, family and friends   08
stand in a circle, cross their arms, hold the hand   09
of the person next to them, and sing "Should   10
auld acquaintance be forgot ...." In Japan, this   11
song is better known as the "time to go home" music in department stores!   12

3 Another Scottish New Year custom is "first footing." Traditionally, the first person to   13
enter your house after midnight should be a dark-haired person carrying gifts such as a   14

piece of coal (to symbolize warmth). These days, people may bring a traditional 15
fruitcake, whisky or other gifts, and they are welcomed with a glass of whisky. This will 16
bring good luck to the house for the coming year. 17

1. Which of the following sentences is true?
   (a) All over Britain, New Year is celebrated in the same way.
   (b) England and Scotland share many New Year customs.
   (c) New Year isn't the biggest annual event in the US.

2. Which of the following does a "custom" mean?
   (a) A person who buys things from a store or from a business
   (b) A traditional style of clothing, often worn in a particular place
   (c) A traditional way of doing something or behaving

3. Which of the following best completes the sentence below?

   A gift of coal shows a hope that _____.

   (a) the family will always have food
   (b) the giver will always be welcome to eat in the house
   (c) the house will never be cold

Your Turn

Festivals and ceremonies are celebrated all over the world. Research and prepare notes about three festivals or ceremonies from outside Japan. Be ready to explain them to your partner(s). Go to page 111 for the worksheet.

Get Ready

Before starting the next unit, look at this important vocabulary. Go to page 112 for the worksheet.

cram school	compulsory	credit	degree	dormitory
economics	elective	graduate	graduate school	job hunting
legal	major	mature	mention	module
politics	postgraduate	scholarship	share	undergraduate

Unit 9

School and University Life

Warm Up

Work with your partner(s). Ask and answer the questions about school and university life. Possible answers are provided. When answering, give additional information. When asking, react and add comments or questions.

1. Which did you enjoy most, elementary school, or junior or senior high school?
   — Probably elementary school. I didn't have to ...

2. What would you most like to change about your university life?
   — I wish I didn't have to ... / I wish we had ... / I wish we could ...

3. What classes are you taking? Which do you like most and which do you like least?
   — I'm taking classes in ... / I enjoy …, but … is really boring!

Vocabulary

This vocabulary will help you talk about school and university life. Complete the sentences below with the words/phrases in the box. Use each word/phrase only once.

compulsory course	credit	elective course	entrance exam
faculty	graduate school	job hunting	junior and senior
major	scholarship		

1. I didn't take the _____. I applied through the Admissions Office.

2. I don't need to take that course if I don't want to. It's a(n) _____.

3. I don't want to get a job just yet. I'm going to go to _____ to get a Master's degree.

4. I'm studying really hard now. If I can get good grades, I'm going to apply for a(n) _____.

5. I'm taking some language courses, but my _____ is business studies.

6. I just need one more _____ to be able to graduate.

7. If I don't pass this course, I'll have to retake it next year. It's a(n) _____.

8. The _____ relationship between students is very important here in Japan.

9. This time of the year is peak _____ season. I've already had five interviews.

10. My professor couldn't meet me because he was in a _____ meeting.

Listening

Before You Listen

Before you listen to Kumi and Danny talking about school and university life, discuss these questions with your partner(s).

1. How do you imagine university life is different in Britain?

_____

2. Is it common for students to share apartments in Japan? If not, why not?

_____

While You Listen

🎧 19

Listen to the conversation and answer these questions.

1. When does the school year start in Britain?

_____

2. How does Danny describe students over the age of 21?

_____

After You Listen

Danny mentioned several differences between Japanese and British universities. How many can you remember? Note each difference with one or two key words such as "campus bars."

_____   _____   _____

_____   _____   _____

_____   _____   _____

Kumi and Danny are chatting over coffee.

Kumi: Danny, you never told me. What are you studying at university?

Danny: I'm doing Asian studies. It's a four-year degree, with the third year spent here in Japan. I can take modules in politics, economics, gender issues, international relations—that kind of thing.

Kumi: Sounds a bit like the degree that I took. Is it a private university?

Danny: No, no! We don't have many private universities. They're almost all public.

Kumi: Really! That's surprising. Have you noticed any big differences between university life here and in Britain?

Danny: Well, campus life is very different—British university campuses all have bars!

Kumi: Oh, of course. The legal drinking age is 18 there, isn't it.

Danny: Yeah … and another difference is that not many students in Britain work part-time. If we work, it's mostly in summer vacation. Oh—and the school year is different—we start our school year in September.

Kumi: Do students live in dormitories?

Danny: Not so much. Maybe for the first year, but after that most students live in shared apartments or houses.

Kumi: What about club activities?

Danny: We have them, but they're not so important. And we don't have a school festival. Oh, one more thing is that we have a lot more mature students than in Japanese universities. In the UK, anyone over 21 is a mature student. Some people on my course are middle-aged or older.

Kumi: That's quite unusual here.

Danny: Yeah, but I think it's really good to have mature students. Oh—and lots of students take gap years—you know, taking a year out to travel or do volunteer work before starting uni. Gap years are very popular in Britain.

Speaking 1 — Talking about Your Student Life

Work in pairs. Imagine your partner is a homestay parent. Answer his/her questions. Always try to give more information and keep the conversation going. Then, change roles.

Homestay parent's questions:

1. What's your university like?
2. What course are you studying and what classes do you take?
3. Do students in your university all live in dormitories?
4. What kind of part-time jobs do students do in Japan?
5. Is there anything you don't enjoy about student life?
6. What do you enjoy most about student life?

Speaking 2 — Overseas Student Interview Project

Do you have international students on campus? If you do, interview at least three students and report back to class. Prepare your questions and practice with your partner before you go to do the interviews. Follow these instructions:

1. Ask the international student to help you with your survey. ("Excuse me, do you have a few minutes? Would you mind helping me with a survey?")
2. Introduce yourself and explain that you are doing a survey for your English class.
3. Ask the student where they are from.
4. Ask them how long they have been studying in Japan, and about their major.
5. Ask them to tell you about any differences that they've experienced between university life in their home country and Japan. Try to find five differences.

After your interviews, try to continue chatting with the student. This activity is a great chance to make new friends!

In class, report your results to your group. For example:
"I interviewed Fernando. He's from Mexico, and he's been here three months. His English was really good. He told me that …"

Wrap Up with Danny

Read the passage and answer the questions below.

1 British students are often surprised by how hard Japanese high school students have   01
to study for university entrance exams. The system in Britain is quite different. High   02
school lasts two years. We have no cram schools, and only a few universities have their   03
own entrance examinations. Instead, in high school we usually choose three or four "A"   04
or "AS" Level courses and take tests only in these subjects. Our coursework and exams   05
are graded from "A*" ("A star") to "E." During the second year of high school, we   06
prepare one application, which is sent to our choice of five universities.   07

2 If our schoolwork, references and predicted "A Level" grades are good enough, we   08
will usually be offered a place at one—or more than one—of the universities. My first   09
choice university offered me a place if I could get "two A's and a B." I actually got an "A,"   10
a "B" and a "C." I phoned them and asked them if I could still come, and they said yes!   11
That was lucky! It's not so easy to get into your first choice university, but it doesn't   12
seem to be as hard as the Japanese system.   13

1. Which of the following sentences is true?
   (a) Danny explains the similarities between Japanese and British high schools.
   (b) Danny outlines how British students apply for university.
   (c) Danny passed his first choice university's entrance exam.

2. Which of the following best completes the sentence below?

"Predicted grades" are _____.

(a) the scores that students are expected to get
(b) the points that universities give to students
(c) the results of entrance exams

3. Which of the following best completes the sentence below?

Danny thinks that the British university entrance system is _____ than the Japanese.

(a) easier   (b) more complicated   (c) shorter

Your Turn

How is school life different in other countries? Choose a country and research its school life. How is it similar to Japan? How is it different? You can research topics such as:

- entrance exams
- school rules
- the school day
- school meals

- school buildings
- school special events
- educational policy
- different ways of learning

Be ready to explain your results to your partner(s). Go to page 113 for the worksheet.

Get Ready

Before starting the next unit, look at this important vocabulary. Go to page 114 for the worksheet.

admire	author	biography	contemporary	director
dramatic	former	influential	inventor	military
period drama	play (a role)	prime minister	scientist	(it's a) shame
slapstick	tearjerker	uplifting	vaccine	well-known

Unit 10

Famous Japanese People and Movies

Warm Up

Work with your partner(s). Ask and answer the questions about famous Japanese people and movies. Possible answers are provided. When answering, give additional information. When asking, react and add comments or questions.

1. Which Japanese people do you think are most famous outside Japan? List at least three.
   — I think … is probably quite well-known. S/he's …

2. Have you ever met a famous person? Tell your partner about the most famous person you've met. If you haven't met a famous person, who would you like to meet, and why?
   — About two years ago I met … S/he was really …
   — I'd really like to meet … I imagine s/he's really …

3. Which famous Japanese people, living or dead, do you most admire, and why?
   — I think Sugihara Chiune was an amazing man. He helped so many people.

4. What's your favorite Japanese movie? What's it about?
   — Do you know the movie …? It's amazing. I've seen it three times! It's …

Vocabulary

A This vocabulary will help you talk about famous people. Make sentences with your partner(s), using the words/phrases in the box below.

author	businessperson	chat show host	chef
former prime minister	inventor	military leader	TV presenter

Example:

(Honda Soichiro) was a <u>businessperson</u>. He (founded Honda Motor Company).

1. (   ) is/was a(n) _____. S/he (   ).

2. (   ) is/was a(n) _____. S/he (   ).

3. (   ) is/was a(n) _____. S/he (   ).

4. (   ) is/was a(n) _____. S/he (   ).

5. (   ) is/was a(n) _____. S/he (   ).

6. (   ) is/was a(n) _____. S/he (   ).

7. (   ) is/was a(n) _____. S/he (   ).

B This vocabulary will help you talk about movies. Japanese cinema has developed a variety of genres. Match each genre to an explanation (1–6).

coming of age	contemporary	gangster
monster	period	sword-fighting

1. *Jidaigeki* (時代劇) are _____ dramas, often set in the Edo era, for example ...

2. *Kaiju eiga* (怪獣映画) are _____ films, such as ...

3. *Seishun eiga* (青春映画) are _____ films about young people, such as ...

4. *Gendaigeki* (現代劇) are _____ movies, such as ...

5. *Chanbara* (チャンバラ) are _____ movies, such as ...

6. *Yakuza eiga* (ヤクザ映画) are _____ movies, such as ...

Listening

Before You Listen

Before you listen to Kayla and Maki talking about famous Japanese people and movies, discuss these questions with your partner(s):

1. Which famous people are featured on Japanese bank bills?

_____

2. Do you know any other people who have appeared on Japanese bank bills in the past?

_____

While You Listen

Listen to the conversation and answer these questions.

1. Who does Maki describe as "very influential in the Meiji era"?

_____

2. What is the English title of *Sen to Chihiro no Kamikakushi* (千と千尋の神隠し)?

_____

After You Listen

Maki mentioned three famous Japanese people. Who were they and what were their occupations?

• _____

• _____

• _____

Conversation

Kayla and Maki are talking about famous Japanese people.

Kayla: So, who are some famous Japanese that I should know about?

Maki: Oh, there are so many. Uhm … do you know Noguchi Hideyo? He was a scientist. I think he discovered a vaccine for yellow fever, maybe in the 1920's?

Kayla: Cool! But no, sorry, I've never heard of him. Anyone else?

Maki: OK … have you heard of Sugihara Chiune? He was a diplomat in the Second World War. I think he was based in Lithuania. Anyway, he gave visas to thousands of Jewish people and that made it possible for them to escape from Europe. He saved their lives.

Kayla: Wow, no, sorry, I've never heard of him either! So he was like a Japanese Schindler?

Maki: Yes, very much like Schindler. I wish more people knew about him. All right, uhm, another one, … Fukuzawa Yukichi. He was an author who was very influential in the Meiji era. He was also a teacher, a translator, an entrepreneur, and a politician—and he

founded Keio University.

Kayla: Wow, sorry again! I'm kind of embarrassed. I think the most famous Japanese person that I've ever heard of is that film director—is it Miyazaki?

Maki: Oh, right, Miyazaki Hayao? Another Japanese hero! Have you seen any of his movies?

Kayla: Yeah—my sister really loves anime, so I watched some with her.

Maki: Which ones did you see?

Kayla: Let's see, uhm, *Totoro*—or *My Neighbour Totoro* in English. *Kiki's Delivery Service*, *Princess Mononoke*, *Spirited Away* …

Maki: *Spirited Away*? Which one's that?

Kayla: It's the one where the little girl is moving house with her parents, and her parents turn into pigs. She has to work in the bathhouse to be able to save them and turn them back into people before they get eaten.

Maki: I loved that movie. Do you know the title in Japanese?

Speaking 1   Guessing the Famous Person

A Your teacher will give you a quiz about famous Japanese people.

If your team guesses the answer after the first hint, score 3 points.
If your team guesses the answer after the second hint, score 2 points.
If your team guesses the answer after the third hint, score 1 point.
If you can't guess the person, the teacher scores 2 points.

B Work in groups. Write quizzes about three famous people, with three hints for each person. Don't make them too easy, and don't make them too hard! Challenge your teacher or another group. For example:

1. This writer was born in Kyoto in 1949.
2. He's one of Japan's greatest novelists.
3. The English title of his best-known work is *Norwegian Wood*.

These expressions will help you make your own quizzes:

S/he's a movie director and an actor.	S/he comes from Yokohama.
S/he's famous for ...	S/he was born in 1950.
S/he was married to ...	S/he starred in ... / S/he appeared in (*TV show or movie title*).
S/he played (*role*) in the movie (*title*).	
Most of his/her movies/songs/books are about ...	Her/His initials are KT. / Her/His family name starts with a "K."
S/he invented/discovered/designed ...	

Speaking 2 Guessing the Movie

Describe a well-known Japanese movie to your partners. Can they guess the title of the movie?

Example 1:

It's about a professional cello player who loses his job. He gets a new job in a funeral business, and he has to prepare dead bodies. His wife isn't happy about this job, but he learns a lot of things about life and death.

Example 2:

This movie is a real tearjerker! It's a romantic drama about two high school classmates. She's suffering from a terminal illness, but she's very positive and tries to enjoy her life. He helps her to experience her bucket list of things to do before she dies. This film was one of the most popular in 2017. It has a strange title but …

Wrap Up with Kayla   🎧 22

Read the passage and answer the questions below.

1 My friend Alex is crazy about Japanese movies, so we watched some together before   01
I came to Japan. And you know what? Some were awful, but some were really   02
interesting. He showed me two by the director Itami Juzo. They were very funny and I   03
learned a lot about Japanese culture, especially about social customs and relationships.   04
One was called *The Funeral*. It was about the efforts of a family to organize a funeral for   05
their father and husband. It made me realize that even Japanese people can have trouble   06
with Japanese etiquette!   07

2 Another movie, *Tanpopo* (タンポポ), helped me to understand the deep relationship that   08
Japanese have with food. It also shows how the delicate balance of social politeness can   09
be upset if you don't follow the unwritten social rules. One scene, where a young office   10
worker goes for lunch with his older colleagues and   11
some guests, was particularly funny.   12

3 These days young people don't usually watch   13
older movies. We just rush to see whatever's new and   14
popular. But when I started watching movies with   15
Alex, I realized that there are so many good older   16
films waiting to be discovered. Can you recommend   17
any?   18

70

1. What does "awful" in Paragraph 1 mean?
   (a) amazing   **(b)** boring   **(c)** terrible

2. How did Kayla find Itami Juzo's films?
   (a) They were culturally very informative.
   (b) They were really awful.
   (c) They were very funny but sad.

3. Which of the following sentences is true?
   (a) Kayla recommends that young office workers go for lunch with their co-workers.
   (b) Kayla suggests that young people should try watching some older movies.
   (c) Kayla wants young people to watch more modern movies.

Your Turn

Get ready to quiz your partner(s) about three "mystery" movies and three famous people. Prepare a short text or notes. Go to page 115 for the worksheet.

Get Ready

Before starting the next unit, look at this important vocabulary. Go to page 116 for the worksheet.

amulet	Buddhism	certificate	chant	deity
evil	fortune-telling	horoscope	lucky charm	memorial ceremony
monk	offering	pray	prayer beads	prayer board
priest	protect	purify	religious	Shinto(ism)

Unit 11
Visiting Temples and Shrines

Warm Up

Work with your partner(s). Ask and answer the questions about temples and shrines. Possible answers are provided. When answering, give additional information. When asking, react and add comments or questions.

1. Do you enjoy visiting temples or shrines? When do you usually visit them?
   — I enjoy visiting the big, famous ones. I usually go in …, or ...

2. Tell your partner about your favorite temples and shrines.
   — I love going to … because ...
   — I really like visiting … It's such a(n) ...

Vocabulary

Ⓐ This vocabulary will help you talk about temples and shrines. The sentences below describe items related to temples and shrines. Complete the descriptions with the words/phrases in the box.

arrows	curved bead	fortune-telling papers	incense	lucky charms
prayer beads	prayer boards	rope	stamps	tablets

1. *Goshuincho*（御朱印帳）is a kind of book for collecting _____ from visits to shrines and temples.

2. *Hamaya* are decorative _____ to protect people from evil. They're sold at New Year.

3. A *shimenawa*（しめ縄）is a kind of twisted straw or hemp _____ that indicates a sacred place.

4. *Juzu*（数珠）are _____; they're on a string, like a bracelet.

5. *Magatama* (勾玉) are amulets shaped like a(n) _____.

6. *Senko* (線香) is _____. It's usually sold in sticks and burnt at graves or temples.

7. *Omamori* (お守り) are _____ that protect people when they travel, drive, etc.

8. *Omikuji* (おみくじ) are _____. We often buy them at the temple or shrine.

9. *Ema* (絵馬) are small _____. We write our prayers and wishes on them.

10. *Ihai* (位牌) are Buddhist memorial _____, for our ancestors' family altars.

B Match the items described above (1–10) to the photos below. Write the words, not the numbers.

a
_____

b
_____

c
_____

d
_____

e
_____

f
_____

g
_____

h
_____

i
_____

j
_____

Listening

Before You Listen

Before you listen to Danny and Maki talking about temples and shrines, discuss these questions with your partner(s):

1. What are the differences between praying at a shrine and praying at a temple?

_____

2. Which do you usually visit more often, temples or shrines? Why?

_____

While You Listen

Listen to the conversation and answer these questions.

1. Apart from the names, how does Maki suggest Danny can tell the difference between a temple and a shrine?

_____

2. Is Maki very religious? How do you know that?

_____

After You Listen

How is it possible for Japanese to follow both Shinto and Buddhism?

_____

Conversation

Maki is showing Danny around one of their local shrines.

Danny: So, I've washed my hands, what do I do here?

Maki: Right, so you drop your money into the offering box, then shake the rope, then bow twice, then clap your hands twice, then bow again.

Danny: Right, OK! Why do you clap your hands?

Maki: I guess for the same reason that we shake the rope to ring the bell. It's to purify the area and to let the *kami* (神) —the deity of the shrine—know that you're here.

Danny: OK. Then I say a prayer, or make a wish?

Maki: That's right. Then bow one more time, then back away, because it's rude to show your back to the gods.

Danny: OK. I'll try to remember that! Do you come here every week?

Maki: No, no, no! Usually only at New Year or when we have something special to pray for. And of course, we like to visit the famous temples and shrines when we go on trips.

Danny: So this is a *Shinto* shrine, right? How can I tell the difference between a shrine and a Buddhist temple?

Maki: Well, the name will help you. If the name ends in *-jinja* (神社) , *-gu* (宮) , *-miya* (宮) , *-jingu* (神宮) or *-taisha* (大社) , it's a shrine, and if it ends in *-tera* (寺) , *-dera* (寺) , *-ji* (寺) or *-in* (院) , it's a temple. And of course, when you see them, shrines have big *torii* (鳥居) entrance gateways, and temples often have statues of monks.

Danny: What about you, Maki? Are you Shintoist or Buddhist?

Maki: Both! Although I must admit I'm not really serious about either. Maybe some people feel it's a little strange, but I think most Japanese feel it's quite natural to follow both Shinto and Buddhism. They're different, but they don't compete with each other.

Danny: So what are the differences between Shinto and Buddhism?

Speaking Temples and Shrines Bingo

Let's play bingo in pairs. Partner A, go to page 91. Partner B, go to page 95. Follow the instructions:

1. Write the numbers 1–25 AT RANDOM in the grid. Don't show your partner your grid.
2. Your partner will say a number between 1 and 25 (for example "7").
3. Explain item "7" in your grid, but DON'T SAY THE WORD! Give as much information as you can.
4. When your partner correctly says the word ("Is it ...?"), circle the number on your bingo card.
5. Keep taking turns until both of you have got Bingo!

Example 1:

A: It's a kind of decorative arrow that we buy at New Year. It's supposed to protect us from bad luck and evil spirits. It's what we call an *engimono* (縁起物) . It's like a lucky charm.

B: Is it *hamaya*?

A: That's right!

Example 2:

A: They're gods or deities. It's their job to guard the temple and to remind people that they should try to be good. They're usually made of wood, and can look very big and scary!

B: Are they *nio* (仁王) ?

A: Well done! Yes, that's right.

Remember!

· Don't use one-word hints. Use complete sentences.

· Give your partner time to explain.

· Ask questions if you need more information.

These expressions will help you explain things to your partner:

It's like a(n) ...

It's something we use to ...

It's something we do/use when we ...

It's a place where we ...

It's a kind of …

It's made of ...

Wrap Up with Danny

24

Read the passage and answer the questions below.

1 I love going round temples and shrines. They feel like the real heart of Japanese 01
culture and tradition, and—if there aren't too many tourists—they're also nice, calm 02
places. I'm sure your visitors will have lots of questions when you visit temples and 03
shrines, and I hope you'll be able to answer them. But visiting places with Maki has 04
taught me that if you want to be a *good* guide for your guest, it's important to do more 05
than just walk around with them. 06

2 Maki was a great guide because she knew the points 07
of interest and was always ready to explain them. I 08
looked at things like *komainu* (狛犬), and took a picture 09
or two, and started walking away. Maki helped me 10
understand more because she actively pointed things 11
out and explained them. Now I can understand the 12
komainu's role in guarding the shrine and I can 13
remember the symbolism of their "*ah-un* (阿吽)" open 14
and closed mouths. I remember the visit much more, 15
and I'm very grateful to Maki for that. 16

3 I hope you can guide your visitors well. Learn about 17
the points of interest and be ready to explain them to 18
your guest. They'll definitely thank you for it! 19

1. Which of the following best completes the sentence below?

   Danny thinks that a good guide should be _____.

   (a) active and well-informed   **(b)** fluent and energetic   **(c)** talkative and calm

2. What does "pointed things out" in Paragraph 2 mean?

   (a) answered a question

   (b) brought something to my attention

   (c) identified a problem and found a solution

3. Which of the following sentences is true?

   (a) Danny learned more about temples and shrines thanks to Maki's explanations.

   (b) Danny enjoys visiting temples and shrines because there are so many tourists.

   (c) Danny finds temples and shrines boring, unless he can take photos.

Your Turn

A pilgrimage is a journey to visit a religious place. Most religions have these special places. Japanese Buddhists, for example, can follow in the footsteps of Kukai (空海), by joining the 88-temple pilgrimage in Shikoku (四国).

Research two pilgrimages from outside Japan. Make notes and be ready to explain them to your partner(s). Go to page 117 for the worksheet. Be sure to talk about:

· where the pilgrimage happens

· when it happens

· how long it takes

· which religious group it is special to

· what pilgrims do on the pilgrimage

Get Ready

Before starting the next unit, look at this important vocabulary. Go to page 118 for the worksheet.

borrow	bullet train	cause	concept	express
expression	fascinating	hesitate	honest	interact
invisible	nonverbal	nuisance	obedient	patience
put up with ...	respect	society	stereotype	values

Unit 12

Invisible Culture

Warm Up

Work with your partner(s). Ask and answer the questions about cultural differences. Possible answers are provided. When answering, give additional information. When asking, react and add comments or questions.

1. Do you think Japanese culture is easy for non-Japanese to understand? Why or why not?
   — Maybe it's quite difficult to understand. Especially because ...

2. What do you think might be difficult for foreigners when they come to live in Japan?
   — ... is probably quite challenging. I imagine it's difficult to ....

Vocabulary

This vocabulary will help you talk about Japan's invisible culture. Complete the sentences below with the words in the box. Use each word only once.

borrowed	concept	express	expression	invisible
nuisance	obedient	patience	stereotypes	values

1. English has _____ thousands of words from French.

2. It's difficult to explain the _____ of *amae* (甘え) without using an example.

3. The _____ *ishin denshin* (以心伝心) explains a lot about Japanese communication style.

4. _____ culture is usually harder to explain than things that we can see.

5. In Japan, being a _____ to other people is a real no-no!

6. Most parents want their children to be honest and _____.

7. The expression "*ishi no ue ni mo san nen* (石の上にも三年)" means that _____

78

is important for success.

8. To really understand a culture, we need to see beyond the _____.

9. In any culture, nonverbal communication is an important way to _____ yourself.

10. _____ such as honesty, hard work and respect often feature in traditional stories.

Listening

Before You Listen

Before you listen to Kumi and Kayla talking about invisible Japanese culture, discuss these questions with your partner(s):

1. What stereotypical images do you think foreign visitors have of Japan?

_____

2. Which is easier to explain, visible or invisible culture? Why?

_____

While You Listen

🎧 25

Listen to the conversation and answer these questions.

1. How does Kayla describe the things that appear in documentaries?

_____

2. What images does Kayla use to describe visible and invisible culture?

_____

After You Listen

What examples of invisible culture did Kayla mention?

_____

Kumi comes home. Kayla is reading a book.

Kumi: Hi Kayla, what are you reading?

Kayla: Oh hi. It's about Japanese culture, but more on the *invisible* culture. It's really interesting.

Kumi: How do you mean?

Kayla: Well, you know, before I came here, I saw some documentaries and they focused on things like monkeys in hot springs, maid cafés, the bullet train, fish markets, geisha, that kind of thing, you know, really stereotypical.

Kumi: Yeah, people love seeing strange and exotic things, right!

Kayla: Yeah, and that's interesting too, but this book is talking about the *invisible* culture. You know, people's values, how they interact, how they communicate.

Kumi: Like what?

Kayla: Like, how some words show what's important in Japanese society. How words like *gaman* (我慢), *gambaru* (がんばる), *meiwaku* (迷惑), *kawaii* (かわいい), *sunao* (素直) tell us a lot about people's values.

Kumi: Mmmm …

Kayla: But not just that. It's explaining about concepts like *kizuna* (絆), *omoiyari* (思いやり), *tatemae* (建前), *enryo* (遠慮) … things that show how people think and how Japanese society works. You know, things like kimono, sushi and so on, the things we can see, these are the *face* of Japan, but the things that we *can't see* are really the heart of Japan.

Kumi: Wow! You're really getting in deep!

Kayla: Yeah, I know! Some people have said that culture is like an iceberg, where 90 percent is invisible to us. It's fascinating, but there's still so much I don't understand. For example, what's *wabisabi* (侘び寂び)?

Speaking 1 Explaining the Concepts

This unit is about how people think and how people act in Japanese society. It focuses on Japan's invisible culture.

Work in pairs. Imagine you are a foreign visitor. Ask your partner what the concepts below mean. Use everyday examples to explain them. When you have finished one of the concepts, change roles.

aimai （曖昧）	*doryoku* （努力）	*enryo* （遠慮）	*giri* （義理）
hikaeme （控えめ）	*sekentei* （世間体）	*ishin denshin* （以心伝心）	*issho kenmei* （一生懸命）
joge kankei （上下関係）	*kikubari* （気配り）	*kyochosei* （協調性）	*ninjo* （人情）
omotenashi （おもてなし）	*oseji* （お世辞）	*reigi* （礼儀）	*sonkei* （尊敬）
sunao （素直）	*tatemae / honne* （建前／本音）	*yuzuriai* （譲り合い）	*wa* （和）

Example 1:

A: What does *omoiyari* mean?

B: *Omoiyari* is a kind of emotional intelligence. It means thinking about another person's situation and acting in the right way. For example, if I'm sitting on a bus, I should think about giving my seat to someone who needs it.

Example 2:

A: What does *gaman* mean?

B: *Gaman* is about accepting a difficult situation when we can't change it. For example, if I want to watch a baseball game, but I promised to do my part-time job and can't change my working time, I have to put up with it. That's *gaman*.

Speaking 2 Understanding Japanese Gestures

Communication isn't only done with words. Understanding and explaining your nonverbal communication is another important skill. While Japanese tend not to use gestures as much as some cultures, there are many Japanese gestures that would not easily be understood by non-Japanese.

Identify and explain the gestures below to your partner(s). For example:

This one is called *maru*. It means "good," "right" or "correct." We sometimes use it when we give the answer to a quiz.

Wrap Up with Kayla

🎧 26

Read the passage and answer the questions below.

1 A little earlier I was talking with Kumi about how words like *gaman, gambaru,* 01
meiwaku, kawaii and *sunao* tell us a lot about people's values. But of course, this doesn't 02
mean that these concepts exist only in Japanese. We can express them all in English 03
too—*gaman* is about "putting up with something," "being stoic," "being patient" or 04
"persevering." *Gambaru* is about "not giving up," or "doing your best." *Meiwaku* is 05
related to "nuisance" or "causing trouble for someone." *Kawaii*, of course, means "cute" 06
and "*sunao*" means "obedient," "easy to influence" or "easy to work with." These are not 07
unique to Japanese society, but what's interesting is that these things are so valued and 08

so often mentioned here. They communicate what is important in Japanese society. 09

2 The same is true of *kizuna*, *omoiyari*, *tatemae* and *enryo*. All these things exist in 10 other cultures, but don't seem to be so important. 11 Of course, sometimes, other cultures realize that a 12 concept *is* important, and that they don't yet have a 13 word for it, so the foreign word will be borrowed to 14 fill the gap. Japanese words such as *boke* (ボケ), *otaku* 15 (オタク), *umami* (旨味) and *hikikomori* (ひきこもり) are all 16 now used in English. Can you think of any others? 17

1. What does "being patient" in Paragraph 1 mean?
   (a) being able to wait, calmly
   (b) being on time, not being late
   (c) not answering when someone asks a question

2. Which of the following best completes the sentence below?

   Kayla says that we can see what is important in a culture by _____.

   (a) translating their expressions into English
   (b) understanding their cultural "key words"
   (c) using Japanese expressions in English

3. Which of the following sentences is true?
   (a) English borrows words from Japanese in the same way that Japanese borrows from English.
   (b) The concept of *sunao* doesn't exist in English culture.
   (c) Words like *gaman* and *gambaru* can't be translated into English.

Your Turn

Learning a foreign language can be an interesting and beautiful experience. We can learn different ways of thinking, and different ways of expressing ourselves. Most languages have their own unique concepts.

Research five "cultural key words" from foreign languages. These words should express concepts that are not easily expressed in Japanese, or that give an insight about that language's culture. Alternatively, research five gestures from other cultures that are not used in Japan. Be ready to explain them to your partner(s). Go to page 119 for the worksheet.

Review Game Units 7–12

Play in groups of three. When it's your turn, play "rock, paper, scissors" with one partner. If you win, move three spaces. If you draw, move two spaces. If you lose, move one space.

Your "rock, paper, scissors" partner should ask you the question on the space where you stopped. Answer the question using complete sentences, not single words. Your second partner should ask you a back-up questions to show interest and get more information.

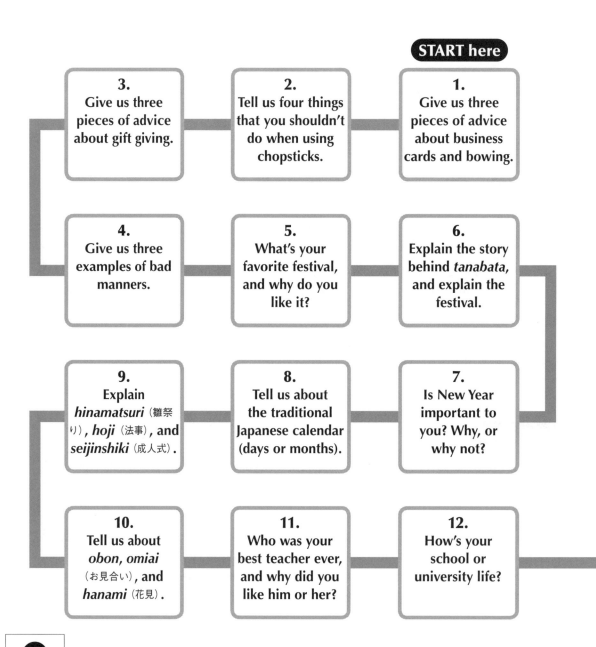

START here

3.
Give us three pieces of advice about gift giving.

2.
Tell us four things that you shouldn't do when using chopsticks.

1.
Give us three pieces of advice about business cards and bowing.

4.
Give us three examples of bad manners.

5.
What's your favorite festival, and why do you like it?

6.
Explain the story behind *tanabata*, and explain the festival.

9.
Explain *hinamatsuri* (雛祭り), *hoji* (法事), and *seijinshiki* (成人式).

8.
Tell us about the traditional Japanese calendar (days or months).

7.
Is New Year important to you? Why, or why not?

10.
Tell us about *obon*, *omiai* (お見合い), and *hanami* (花見).

11.
Who was your best teacher ever, and why did you like him or her?

12.
How's your school or university life?

30.
Explain the concepts of *joge kankei* (上下関係), *issho kenmei,* and *sunao.*

29.
Explain the concepts of *ishin denshin, doryoku,* and *omotenashi.*

28.
Explain three typically Japanese gestures.

25.
Explain four things that you can see at temples or shrines.

26.
Explain what to do before you pray at a shrine.

27.
How can you tell the difference between temples and shrines?

24.
Explain four items that you can buy at temples and shrines.

23.
When do you usually visit temples and shrines, and why?

22.
Where's your favorite temple and favorite shrine?

19.
Tell us about your favorite Japanese movie.

20.
Tell us about your favorite Japanese actors.

21.
What Japanese movies would you recommend, and why?

18.
Name two of the people on Japanese bank bills. Why were they famous?

17.
Tell us about two famous Japanese that you admire.

16.
Talk about your course and tell us five subjects that you're studying.

13.
What are you planning or hoping to do after you graduate?

14.
What would you most like to change about your school or university life?

15.
What clubs do you have in your school or university? List at least five.

Appendix

Appendix I: Communication Bingo Grids

Appendix II: Worksheets for Your Turn and Get Ready

tempura （天ぷら）	kushimono （串物）	makizushi （巻き寿司）	mirin （味りん）	miso （味噌）
karei （カレイ）	tsukemono （漬物）	katsudon （カツ丼）	chahan （チャーハン）	katsuobushi （鰹節）
chikuwa （ちくわ）	fugu （フグ）	tonjiru （豚汁）	karashi （辛子）	chankonabe （ちゃんこ鍋）
chirashizushi （ちらし寿司）	basashi （馬刺し）	daikon （ダイコン）	shoyu （醤油）	inago no tsukudani （イナゴの佃煮）
gobo （ゴボウ）	aonori （青海苔）	kazunoko （数の子）	shochu （焼酎）	goma （ゴマ）

It's something
we use to ...

It's something we
wear when ...

It's a kind of ...

banzai (万歳)	byobu (屏風)	teruterubozu (てるてる坊主)	chindonya (チンドン屋)	junihitoe (十二単)
umi no ie (海の家)	chabudai (ちゃぶ台)	chasen (茶筅)	chozuya (手水舎)	shisetsu oendan (私設応援団)
demae (出前)	fude (筆)	fundoshi (ふんどし)	furisode (振袖)	furoshiki (風呂敷)
tawashi (たわし)	geta (下駄)	engawa (縁側)	haori hakama (羽織袴)	happi (法被)
hashi-oki (箸置き)	hibachi (火鉢)	hyosatsu (表札)	inkan / hanko (印鑑／はんこ)	rakugo (落語)

It's a time when we ...

It's the old name for ...

It's a special day when ...

It's a traditional custom, where we ...

obon （お盆）	taue （田植え）	omisoka （大晦日）	tomobiki （友引）	Koshien （甲子園）
tsukimi （月見）	hakamairi （墓参り）	hanami （花見）	okuizome （お食い初め）	midori no hi （みどりの日）
ohigan / shunbun no hi （お彼岸／春分の日）	shusen kinenbi （終戦記念日）	tenno tanjobi （天皇誕生日）	shochumimai （暑中見舞い）	oseibo （お歳暮）
kekkonshiki （結婚式）	keiro no hi （敬老の日）	kenpo kinenbi （憲法記念日）	kinrokansha no hi （勤労感謝の日）	koromogae （衣替え）
bonenkai （忘年会）	danpatsushiki （断髪式）	Golden Week （ゴールデンウィーク）	choyo no sekku （重陽の節句）	jichinsai （地鎮祭）

It's something we use to ...

It's a place where we ...

It's a kind of ...

danka （檀家）	bonsho （梵鐘）	daikyo （大凶）	ema （絵馬）	gojunoto （五重塔）
haiden （拝殿）	hana-mifuda （花御札）	honden (shinden) （本殿［神殿]）	inari （稲荷）	jizo （地蔵）
kannushi （神主）	komainu (shishi / shisa) （狛犬［獅子／ シーサー]）	manji （卍）	myojin （明神）	oharai （お祓い）
okyo （お経）	omikoshi （お神輿）	joya no kane （除夜の鐘）	otsuya （お通夜）	sakaki （榊）
shaku （釈）	shichifukujin （七福神）	shimenawa （しめ縄）	suzu （鈴）	torii （鳥居）

It's a kind of ...

It's something we use to ...

It's a popular winter dish. We ...

dango （団子）	takoyaki （たこ焼き）	nagashi somen （流しそうめん）	wasabi （ワサビ）	udon （うどん）
soba （そば）	anago （アナゴ）	tarako （タラコ）	nikujaga （肉じゃが）	sukiyaki （すき焼き）
yosemono （寄せ物）	inarizushi （いなり寿司）	okonomiyaki （お好み焼き）	shichimi （七味）	shiokara （塩辛）
natto （納豆）	nigirizushi （にぎり寿司）	shojin ryori （精進料理）	osechi ryori （おせち料理）	shoga （生姜）
onigiri （おにぎり）	oden （おでん）	nimono （煮物）	oyakodon （親子丼）	ramen （ラーメン）

It's something we use to ...

It's a kind of ...

It's something we wear when ...

jikatabi (地下足袋)	jimbei (甚平)	kotatsu (こたつ)	kadomatsu (門松)	kairo (懐炉)
manzai (漫才)	kamon (家紋)	kappa (合羽)	kappogi (割烹着)	saramawashi (皿まわし)
koban (小判)	koinobori (鯉のぼり)	manekineko (招き猫)	masu (升)	meishi (名刺)
mimikaki (耳かき)	mochitsuki (餅つき)	nengajo (年賀状)	noren (暖簾)	bento (弁当)
obi (帯)	chawan (茶碗)	oni (鬼)	sento (銭湯)	oshibori (おしぼり)

It's a traditional custom, where we ...

It's a special day when ...

It's a time when we ...

It's the old name for ...

bunka no hi (文化の日)	tanabata (七夕)	hinamatsuri (雛祭り)	genbaku kinenbi (原爆記念日)	yayoi (弥生)
sotsugyoshiki (卒業式)	kenkoku kinen no hi (建国記念の日)	taian (大安)	sports no hi (スポーツの日)	umi no hi (海の日)
shiwasu (師走)	soshiki (葬式)	kanreki (還暦)	White Day (ホワイトデー)	shogatsu (正月)
kisaragi (如月)	seijinshiki (成人式)	setsubun (節分)	toji (冬至)	shichi-go-san (七五三)
kodomo no hi (こどもの日)	omiai (お見合い)	doyo no ushi no hi (土用の丑の日)	nyugakushiki (入学式)	gokon (合コン)

It's something we use to ...

It's a place where we ...

It's a kind of ...

butsudan （仏壇）	daikichi （大吉）	doso （土葬）	monzenmachi （門前町）	ennichi （縁日）
dashi （山車）	hoji （法事）	ihai （位牌）	ishidoro （石灯籠）	juzu （数珠）
kaso （火葬）	keidai （境内）	miko （巫女）	ofuda （お札）	*Kojiki* （古事記）
omamori （お守り）	omikuji （おみくじ）	omiyamairi （お宮参り）	saisenbako （賽銭箱）	sando （参道）
hatsumode （初詣）	shikishi （色紙）	sotoba （卒塔婆）	tanuki （狸）	yaoyorozu （八百万）

Introduction

Check (✓) the words you already know and look up any words that you don't know to write their meanings in the blanks.

adjective	☐		grin	☐	
anxious	☐		heavy-set	☐	
appearance	☐		idiot	☐	
bald	☐		keen (on)	☐	
beard	☐		look alike	☐	
brother-in-law	☐		occupation	☐	
definitely	☐		outgoing	☐	
department	☐		personality	☐	
describe	☐		petite	☐	
gran	☐		the black sheep (of the family)	☐	

Unit 1 Getting to Know You

Your Turn

Choose one of these activities. Be ready to explain your chosen topic to your partner(s).

(a) What do you know about your family history? Make a family tree.

Example:

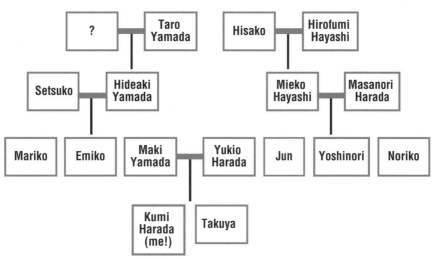

(b) Find some old family photos and explain them to your partner(s).

Example:

This is a picture of my great-grandparents' wedding. I think it's the oldest photo that we have in our family. I'm guessing it was taken sometime around 1925. It's interesting because the little boy in the photo was my great-grandfather's son. This was my great-grandfather's second marriage, because his first wife died. I think they met because they went to the same church. The man with the

mustache is my great-great-grandfather. What do you think of the clothes they wore?

Student ID: _____   **Name:** _____

Your chosen topic (Circle either one): **(a)** / **(b)**

Get Ready   for Unit 2

Check (✓) the words you already know and look up any words that you don't know to write their meanings in the blanks.

agriculture	☐		landslide	☐	
climate	☐		natural disaster	☐	
coast	☐		prefecture	☐	
delicacy	☐		region	☐	
dialect	☐		rural	☐	
earthquake	☐		shrine	☐	
historic	☐		surrounding area	☐	
hot spring	☐		temple	☐	
industry	☐		volcano	☐	
inland	☐		weird	☐	

Unit 2 My Hometown

Your Turn

Have you ever lived abroad? If you have, get ready to introduce your overseas "hometown" to your partner(s). Talk about its location, popular places, climate, main industries, famous food, sports teams, etc. If you've never lived or stayed overseas for a long period, choose an interesting town or city (maybe somewhere a little unusual that you'd like to visit?), research it, and introduce it to your partner(s).

Example:

I've never lived overseas, so I decided to research a place that I really want to visit. The city is called Valletta, and it's in Malta. Malta is an island in the Mediterranean. The old part of the city is a very popular place with tourists. It's very historic, and it has beautiful walls going all round the city. The views of the sea and the harbor are really amazing.

The food there is typical Mediterranean food. One of their famous dishes is a deep-fried rice ball called *arancini*. There are lots of interesting places to visit on the island. One is the 16th-century Lazaretto. It's a place where sailors arriving in Malta would have to stay in quarantine, to show they weren't bringing disease into the country.

Student ID: _____   **Name:** _____

Get Ready for Unit 3

Check (✓) the words you already know and look up any words that you don't know to write their meanings in the blanks.

can't stand	☐		rubbery	☐	
crisp(y)	☐		seasonal	☐	
delicacy	☐		seasoning	☐	
disgusting	☐		seaweed	☐	
fermented	☐		slimy	☐	
fussy eater	☐		steam	☐	
ingredients	☐		sticky	☐	
nutrition	☐		stuff	☐	
presentation	☐		tender	☐	
raw	☐		texture	☐	

Unit 3 Japanese Food

Your Turn

Get ready to introduce three foreign dishes to your partner. Research online to find some tasty and interesting dishes. Do not choose dishes that your partner will certainly know (such as pizza or curry). Be sure to explain the main ingredients and how the dish is made.

Example:

Beshbarmak is the national dish of the Kyrgyz Republic. The name *beshbarmak* means "five fingers." It has this name because traditionally, people ate it with their fingers. It's a noodle dish made by adding boiled, chopped meat—sometimes horsemeat, but usually lamb or mutton—to noodles. It's eaten on special occasions, and is usually served with a kind of onion soup or broth.

Student ID: _____   **Name:** _____

Check (✓) the words you already know and look up any words that you don't know to write their meanings in the blanks.

altar	☐		residential area	☐	
draughty	☐		scroll	☐	
feature	☐		shelf	☐	
last (a long time)	☐		squat	☐	
layout	☐		storage space	☐	
materials	☐		straw	☐	
pillar	☐		suburbs	☐	
prefer	☐		thatched roof	☐	
proper	☐		veranda	☐	
renovate	☐		woven	☐	

Unit 4 The Traditional Japanese House

Your Turn

Choose one of these activities. Be ready to explain your chosen topic to your partner(s).

(a) Think about your dream house. What would it look like? What special features would you like it to have?

Example:

Well, to start with, I'd like to have quite a big house. I want to have plenty of space inside the house and outside. I'd like my house to have high ceilings and a spiral staircase, because I think that looks really cool! I want it to be not too close to other houses, because I want to be able to play music without bothering the neighbors, and I also want an outside area so that I can barbecue with friends and family. I want to be able to see a nice view too, ideally a sunset view over the sea. I know it sounds greedy, but it *is* my ideal house!

(b) Research four differences between Japanese-style houses and western-style houses.

Example:

British houses are usually made of brick or stone, but Japanese houses are usually built using a wooden frame or using reinforced concrete.

Student ID: _____   **Name:** _____

Your chosen topic (Circle either one): **(a)** / **(b)**

Check (✓) the words you already know and look up any words that you don't know to write their meanings in the blanks.

adjective	☐		particle	☐	
adverb	☐		phonetic	☐	
bother	☐		pronunciation	☐	
character	☐		rhythm	☐	
combination	☐		stress	☐	
consonant	☐		stroke order	☐	
flea	☐		syllable	☐	
look something up	☐		verb	☐	
memorize	☐		vowel	☐	
noun	☐		word ending	☐	

Unit 5 The Japanese Language

Your Turn

Learn about a writing system from another culture. Make sure you can understand the sounds and be ready to explain it to your partner(s). It's easier if you use a chart or an illustration.

Example:

Hangul

Hangul is the Korean alphabet. It's been used since the 15th century. Basically it has only 24 letters, and these are 14 consonants and 10 vowels. It's easy to learn Hangul because there aren't so many letters, and the combinations are very logical. On my chart, the top part shows the consonants, and the bottom part shows the vowels. The parts combine to make the sounds, for example …

Student ID: _____   **Name:** _____

Get Ready for Unit 6

Check (✓) the words you already know and look up any words that you don't know to write their meanings in the blanks.

beckon	☐		light	☐	
calligraphy	☐		pack	☐	
cheap	☐		paw	☐	
customer	☐		scoop	☐	
earwax	☐		souvenir	☐	
expensive	☐		suitable	☐	
fan	☐		sword	☐	
fold	☐		traditional	☐	
lacquer	☐		weapon	☐	
lantern	☐		wrap	☐	

Unit 6 Explaining Japanese Things

Your Turn

Kayla talked about the very formal clothes that are needed for Japanese weddings and funerals. What about other cultures and other religions? Research wedding and funeral customs from another culture. Write four points for each ceremony. Be ready to explain them to your partner(s).

Example:

In Britain, the wedding reception is quite different from a Japanese wedding. The bride and groom's parents will sit at the top table, with the bride and groom, and with the chief bridesmaid and the best man. The best man is usually the groom's best friend. The best man has a very important role. He has to make sure that the wedding day goes smoothly, he has to help to take care of the guests, and he also has to make a funny speech at the wedding reception. In British weddings, we don't usually invite our boss, just family and friends. There are usually only three speeches—the groom, the bride's father, and the best man, and these speeches come after the meal, not before it.

Student ID: _____   **Name:** _____

Get Ready for Unit 7

Check (✓) the words you already know and look up any words that you don't know to write their meanings in the blanks.

accidentally	☐		habit	☐	
appropriate	☐		incense	☐	
avoid	☐		lick	☐	
complain	☐		on purpose	☐	
complicated	☐		permission	☐	
confusing	☐		spear	☐	
decorative	☐		stab	☐	
drag	☐		superstition	☐	
funeral	☐		table manners	☐	
grave	☐		tear	☐	

Unit 7 Good Manners, Bad Manners

Your Turn

Research and make notes about three examples of good or bad manners from non-Japanese cultures. Be ready to explain them to your partner(s).

Example:

Many Muslims say *Bismillah* (In the name of God) before eating, and a short prayer *Alhamdulillah* (Thanks be to God) after the meal.

In China, many people are superstitious about flipping a fish over when you've eaten one side. When you finish one side, you should just take out the bones and continue eating.

In Thailand, it's bad manners to point the soles of your feet at people, because the feet are considered to be not very clean. You should also avoid touching people on the head, because the head is a special part of the body.

Student ID: _____   **Name:** _____

Get Ready for Unit 8

Check (✓) the words you already know and look up any words that you don't know to write their meanings in the blanks.

according to ...	☐		equinox	☐	
ancestor	☐		fireworks	☐	
branch	☐		foundation	☐	
ceremony	☐		labor	☐	
coming of age	☐		legend	☐	
commemorate	☐		lunar	☐	
constitution	☐		purify	☐	
custom	☐		ritual	☐	
decorate	☐		wild boar	☐	
display	☐		zodiac	☐	

Unit 8 Special Days and Events

Your Turn

Festivals and ceremonies are celebrated all over the world. Research and prepare notes about three festivals or ceremonies from outside Japan. Be ready to explain them to your partner(s).

Example:

Holi is a festival held every year in spring in India and Nepal. It's usually held on the first full moon in March, but may also be held in late February. It's a Hindu festival to celebrate the victory of good over evil, but it's not a religious festival. People of all social classes enjoy throwing brightly-colored powder at each other. It doesn't matter whether they are rich or poor, if they are friends or strangers, you can throw powder at anyone. They also enjoy singing and dancing. The festival is also known as "the festival of color" or "the festival of love."

Student ID: _____   **Name:** _____

Get Ready for Unit 9

Check (✓) the words you already know and look up any words that you don't know to write their meanings in the blanks.

cram school	☐		legal	☐	
compulsory	☐		major	☐	
credit	☐		mature	☐	
degree	☐		mention	☐	
dormitory	☐		module	☐	
economics	☐		politics	☐	
elective	☐		postgraduate	☐	
graduate	☐		scholarship	☐	
graduate school	☐		share	☐	
job hunting	☐		undergraduate	☐	

Unit 9 School and University Life

Your Turn

How is school life different in other countries? Choose a country and research its school life. How is it similar to Japan? How is it different? You can research topics such as:

- entrance exams
- school rules
- the school day
- school meals

- school buildings
- school special events
- educational policy
- different ways of learning

Be ready to explain your results to your partner(s).

Example:

I researched school life in Costa Rica. Costa Rica is in Central America. Its education system has a very good reputation. Maybe it's a little unusual, because the school year starts in February and ends in December. Students get a two-month holiday at the end of the year and another long holiday in July. Students all have to wear uniforms, at least until high school (which they call "college"). Class sizes are quite small, usually below 30, and apart from Spanish and math, English and computer science are very important. Literacy rates are very high in Costa Rica, and the best thing? It's that public education is free!

Student ID: _____   **Name:** _____

Get Ready for Unit 10

Check (✓) the words you already know and look up any words that you don't know to write their meanings in the blanks.

admire	☐		period drama	☐	
author	☐		play (a role)	☐	
biography	☐		prime minister	☐	
contemporary	☐		scientist	☐	
director	☐		(it's a) shame	☐	
dramatic	☐		slapstick	☐	
former	☐		tearjerker	☐	
influential	☐		uplifting	☐	
inventor	☐		vaccine	☐	
military	☐		well-known	☐	

Unit 10 Famous Japanese People and Movies

Your Turn

Get ready to quiz your partner(s) about three "mystery" movies and three famous people. Prepare a short text or notes.

These expressions will help you describe the mystery movies:

It's set in Tokyo. / It's set in the 1930's.

It was made in 2020.

It stars Tom Hanks.

It's based on a novel by Haruki Murakami.

It's based on a true story.

It was directed by Takeshi Kitano.

It's about a woman/man who …

It's a   period/costume drama.

horror movie.

feel-good movie.

sci-fi (science fiction) movie.

psycho-thriller.

documentary.

rom-com (romantic comedy).

tearjerker.

It's an action movie.

animation/animated movie.

Example:

This movie is set in Tokyo, and it's about a family who survive by stealing things from shops. They take care of a young girl who they find in the street. It's an interesting film because it makes you think about what's right and what's wrong with society's values. It's very moving, and has a powerful ending. It was directed by Hirokazu Koreeda in 2018, and won the best film award at the 2018 Cannes Film Festival.

Student ID: _____   **Name:** _____

Get Ready for Unit 11

Check (✓) the words you already know and look up any words that you don't know to write their meanings in the blanks.

amulet	☐		monk	☐	
Buddhism	☐		offering	☐	
certificate	☐		pray	☐	
chant	☐		prayer beads	☐	
deity	☐		prayer board	☐	
evil	☐		priest	☐	
fortune-telling	☐		protect	☐	
horoscope	☐		purify	☐	
lucky charm	☐		religious	☐	
memorial ceremony	☐		Shinto(ism)	☐	

Unit 11 Visiting Temples and Shrines

Your Turn

A pilgrimage is a journey to visit a religious place. Most religions have these special places. Japanese Buddhists, for example, can follow in the footsteps of Kukai (空海), by joining the 88-temple pilgrimage in Shikoku (四国).

Research two pilgrimages from outside Japan. Make notes and be ready to explain them to your partner(s). Be sure to talk about:

- where the pilgrimage happens
- when it happens
- how long it takes
- which religious group it is special to
- what pilgrims do on the pilgrimage

Example:

Adam's Peak in Sri Lanka

Adam's Peak (*Sri Pada*) is a mountain in Sri Lanka. At the top of the mountain there's a sacred footprint. Some Christians and some Muslims believe it's the footprint of Adam, when he stepped down from heaven. Some Buddhists believe it is the footprint of the Buddha. Some Hindus believe it is the footprint of Shiva. Pilgrims climb 5,000–6,000 steps to pray at the top of the 2,200-meter-high mountain. It takes about two to four hours to climb to the top.

Student ID: _____   **Name:** _____

Check (✓) the words you already know and look up any words that you don't know to write their meanings in the blanks.

borrow	☐		invisible	☐	
bullet train	☐		nonverbal	☐	
cause	☐		nuisance	☐	
concept	☐		obedient	☐	
express	☐		patience	☐	
expression	☐		put up with ...	☐	
fascinating	☐		respect	☐	
hesitate	☐		society	☐	
honest	☐		stereotype	☐	
interact	☐		values	☐	

Unit 12 Invisible Culture

Your Turn

Learning a foreign language can be an interesting and beautiful experience. We can learn different ways of thinking, and different ways of expressing ourselves. Most languages have their own unique concepts.

Research five "cultural key words" from foreign languages. These words should express concepts that are not easily expressed in Japanese, or that give an insight about that language's culture. Alternatively, research five gestures from other cultures that are not used in Japan. Be ready to explain them to your partner(s).

Example:

- *Hygge* is a Danish word to express the nice feeling of coziness and warmth, for example, sitting around a fire with good friends in winter.
- *Schadenfreude* is German word to express the feeling of finding happiness in other people's misfortune.
- *Saudade* is a Portuguese word to communicate feelings of sadness, nostalgia or longing for something that you may never be able to experience again.
- *Ubuntu* is a Zulu word to express a shared compassion and humanity, to communicate how we are all connected.

Student ID: _____   **Name:** _____

クラス用音声 CD 有り（別売）

This Is Japan, New Edition
Your Culture, Your Life

英語で伝える日本の文化と生活

2021 年 1 月 20 日　初版発行
2024 年 1 月 20 日　第 5 刷

著　　者	Simon Capper
発 行 者	松村達生
発 行 所	センゲージ ラーニング株式会社

〒 102-0073　東京都千代田区九段北 1-11-11　第 2 フナトビル 5 階
電話　03-3511-4392
FAX　03-3511-4391
e-mail: eltjapan@cengage.com
copyright © 2021 センゲージ ラーニング株式会社

装　　丁	森村直美
組　　版	有限会社トライアングル
イラスト	湊　敦子
印刷・製本	株式会社平河工業社

ISBN 978-4-86312-383-0